Contents

I Want To Be Me!

To be your natural self, to find your primary talent and make the most of your life can take many twists and turns and years to achieve. Many people spend their whole life on this journey, getting side-tracked or stopping completely, never reaching their destination.

This is because there are so many barriers preventing us from achieving our potential, from being the magnificent human beings we are meant to be.

These obstacles are on the outside and inside of us.

Our parents, teachers, bosses tell us what to do. The outer world is very influential. (Think of all the newspapers, magazines, film and television programmes, governments, religions, clubs and groups that tell you how you should look, behave and what you should aspire to.)

We are pressurised into making choices that go against our grain until we can no longer feel or see our truth.

The world today values technological progress, money and material success, yet we understand our work-life balance is out of kilter. It feels like we are on an ever faster train without brakes, about to hit the buffers at journey's end.

We have a growing sense of unease that underneath the rush, blur and speed of life, we are not really *living*. This makes us anxious, stressed, burnt out to the point where we feel like dropping out and making rash decisions we may come to regret.

To be true to ourselves, to find our talent and purpose and live an authentic life seems like a huge mountain to climb. Even if we don't use the outer world as an excuse not to be who we are, our inner-world of self-doubt, fear, lack of confidence, lack of self-love, vanity, pride and ego causes us to look for problems rather than solutions, to think of reasons why not to act rather than to take action.

So, we 'cope our way through life'. Is this any better than 'sleep-walking', finding ourselves at the end of our lives looking back on all the dreams and missed opportunities, so full of regrets?

You **can** do something. Start by making a little time in your busy life to relax, reflect and regenerate. The 360 Wisdom Guide will help you to 'come off the pace', to explore your inner-world. It will help you to understand *you* and what you are capable of. Then you can decide how you want to realise this outside of the 'self' in the world.

The model to help you in the 360 Wisdom Guide is called '360 Wisdom'. It provides you with a holistic blue-print for living and working today.

360 Wisdom can be applied to any life situation by people of all ages, backgrounds and abilities.

Whether you have a relationship you need to understand better or improve, a problem to solve or something you need to understand in yourself, the 360 Wisdom Guide is designed to help you move forward and get on with your life.

All you need is the curiosity and willingness to have a go at the exercises in this Guide and absorb its stories and ideas. Then you can apply the ones most useful to you in your daily life. The 360 Wisdom Guide has space for you to write down your findings from the exercises, your ideas and illuminating thoughts. There will be suggestions made about other reading material, courses and daily practice to deepen your learning.

By blending all my working experience leading teams, coaching and mentoring individuals with many years of studying business, creativity and spiritual thinking, I've gained the wisdom that the art of living is to know and believe in yourself and the goodness of others, no matter what knocks and setbacks life sometimes brings.

I am reminded of this quote by John M. Richardson," When it comes to the future there are three kinds of people: those who let it happen, those who make it happen, and those who wonder what happened." (1)

So, let's get cracking. Turn to the Introduction and make a start. Be the one who makes it happen!

Claire Chidley February 2011.

What Do the Symbols Mean?

As you work through this Guide, you'll notice a number of features, highlighted by the following symbols:

Write. Exercises that ask you to make notes on something, find out information or practice a task.

Think. Exercises that ask you to take time out to consider your views on an issue/idea.

Look. View a speech or lecture.

Listen. To a guided visualisation or speech. (These can be found on www.360wisdom.co.uk and clicking on '360 Wisdom Guided Visualisation'.)

Feel. To observe and feel emotions or feelings inside you and towards others.

You can use the 'My Notes' section at the back of the Guide for any ideas and reflections you may have.

Introducing the 360 Wisdom Model

Tony

Tony is a successful Solicitor in his early 50's who likes order and predictability. His parents instilled in him that a good education followed by hard work would bring the success and recognition he currently has.

- He has lots of acquaintances, no close friends and nobody special in his life.
- He thinks artists are people with weak minds and loose morals.
- He believes when you are dead that's it. Religion and spirituality is mumbo-jumbo.

Fiona

Fiona is a social worker aged 39. She's married with four children.

- Her clients and family are more important than anything.
- Her heart rules her head.
- She champions lost causes.
- She hasn't got time for hobbies or entertainment.
- Money isn't important. She spends it, lends it or gives it away.
- Last year, she walked the Great Wall of China for charity.

Carol

Carol is a 27-year-old single mum of two. She works at her children's school.

- Her home is colourful and vibrant. She cooks meals from scratch, using fruit and vegetables grown on her allotment.
- She has lots of business ideas but somehow they never get off the ground.
- Her relationships with men are short and end theatrically.
- She wants to take up yoga and meditation but hasn't got round to it yet.

Bridget

Bridget is a successful, 66-year-old businesswoman who is just about to retire.

- She inherited a tea plantation and turned it into an organic, Fair-trade company.
- She is loved by her employees who find her a fair, compassionate boss.
- She reads mystical writings in between her daily practice of tai chi.
- She is setting up a trust fund for young people in business.
- She lives alone preferring the company of animals to people.

Each person has something they do well.

Tony is rich and successful.

Fiona is compassionate and empathetic.

Carol creates beautiful things.

Bridget makes a difference and wants to leave the world a better place.

Whilst they all have a clear strength, they also have aspects of their character and personality that could be improved.

- Tony finds it hard to make emotional connections. He'd really like to find a partner to share his life.
- Fiona lacks time to herself. She'd like to have a relaxing hobby like watercolour painting.
- Carol has ideas but never turns them into practical outcomes. She'd really like some help to set up a business baking and selling cakes.
- Bridget's desire to be alone is making her out of touch with a world where she wants to leave her 'mark'.

Whilst these may be stereotypical examples, (for in reality, we have elements of each of these characters within us to greater or lesser degrees,) the strengths and weaknesses Tony, Fiona, Carol, and Bridget possess represent the four 'Quarters' of the 360 Wisdom Circle™.

The 360 Wisdom Circle

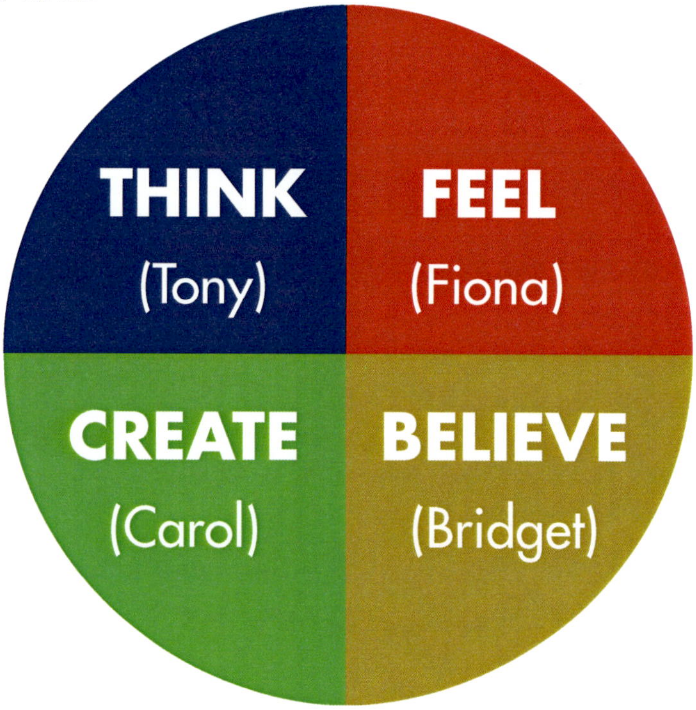

The quarters are:

- **THINK** Thinking for yourself and recognising your thinking patterns and their origin.
- **FEEL** Being emotionally expressive, compassionate, aware of yourself and the perspective of others. Managing yourself, your relationships in your inner and outer worlds.
- **CREATE** Your creative expression and use of imagination. The ability to generate new ideas and possibilities. To dream. To know and appreciate beauty.
- **BELIEVE** The journey of self-improvement. To find the joy in life and your purpose.

THINK, **FEEL**, **CREATE**, and **BELIEVE** have been flagged with the primary colours red, blue and yellow and the secondary colour green to help you remember the Quarters.

Each person has strengths in one quarter called the Home Quarter. When you know what your Home Quarter is, you can work out how to use it more purposefully in your life as well as develop a better understanding of the areas you are less competent in. The Quarters for improvement are called Away Quarters.

You Gain 360 Wisdom From Two Main Routes

1. Sharing your expertise and knowledge in your strongest 'Home Quarter' with others and receiving their expertise in return.
2. Building up your 'Away Quarters' through self-development, learning by experience and contemplation.

So, if Tony could gain a bit of Fiona's emotional connectivity, then Tony could help Carol be more focused and businesslike. Carol could help Fiona relax through creative pursuits and all of them could help shape Bridget's dream and legacy to help others realise their potential.

They could bring in specialists to fill the gaps or they could try to be more adept themselves by learning about the other Quarters and practicing how to become proficient in them while incorporating them into their daily life. Interacting with people who are different to you is an important part of the journey to becoming 360-aware.

Working with others who have different Home Quarters to your own will help you grow and become balanced. Over time, the person who integrates **THINK, FEEL, CREATE** and **BELIEVE** into their life will see the connections between things, be able to create their future and live an enriched, holistic life.

Travelling Around the 360 Wisdom Circle

Section One of the **360 Wisdom Guide** helps you identify your Home and Away Quarters.

Section Two provides a brief overview about the Ranges.

Sections Three, Four, Five and Six take you on a journey around the 360 Wisdom Circle.

You explore each Quarter in turn to experience a greater depth of understanding about THINK, FEEL CREATE and BELIEVE with specific information about the Ranges and how you can live healthily in each Quarter.

The Journey

Soon, you will become familiar with the Quarters. You will understand your Home Quarter and ways to build up your capability in your Away Quarters. You will learn to live within them in a Healthy Range. With your new-found understanding and knowledge, you can evaluate, make new and different choices in your life, generating more options to solve problems and create more opportunities.

Section Seven introduces the concept of 'Crystallisation' and how your changed self-awareness offers you choice in your decision making.

After Crystallisation takes place, you can position yourself at the centre of the 360 Wisdom Circle at will on the Diamond (see page 65).

Section Eight explains how to work from the Diamond with 360 Wisdom for the world.

There, you enjoy a far deeper dimension of reality. This is 360 WISDOM, where anything and everything is possible and can happen.

Section One: Home and Away Quarters

The first thing to recognise is your 'Home Quarter'. Most people have one, a place of both comfort and strength. A Home Quarter is the natural style that flows from within you. You are born into the world with a preference which can be turned into a talent under the right conditions. This is your 'gift' to share with the world to improve the life on this planet. When people reconnect with their Home Quarter or find it for the first time, they say "It's like coming home" (hence the name *Home* Quarter).

Right from an early age, Carol used to sit drawing and experimenting with colour, before she could write and read. Tony was fascinated by figures and equations. He liked the purity of numbers. They were like a new language that he could understand.

Yet, in adulthood, neither Tony nor Carol play to these strengths or even consciously know what they are.

The first thing is to know your Home Quarter, for this is your core strength.

Within this context, it's easy to 'mis-type' your Home Quarter because modern living has caused us to forget or lose touch with who we really are. So, 360 Wisdom has a range of exercises to test you from a number of angles so you can be sure of your Home Quarter.

Carol always wanted to study fine art, but her Mother told her painting wasn't a proper job and sent her to secretarial college. She found she could still express her creative side in the way she dressed herself and her home, but it took a long time before she could make use of her creativity. Now she works in school helping small children create art, explaining to their parents how their talent should be used, not wasted.

Tony was encouraged by his parents into a 'thinking career' that, on the one hand, played to his Home Quarter, but he would have liked to have done something with finance, e.g., become an Actuary or an Accountant and start up his own business.

Adapting Your Self

Your Home Quarter can be shaped by the education you've had or the job you do but it isn't defined by it. Sometimes your life choices have you doing completely the opposite to your Home Quarter because your responsibilities for your family, work, friends, have meant you have to prioritise other things as Carol has for most of her life.

Likewise Bridget inherited someone else's business (the Tea Plantation). She could have sold it or got someone else to run it, but her sense of BELIEF meant she understood she had a wider responsibility to the workers and the community. She chose to *adapt* the external environment to her Home Quarter. Over the years, she gradually shaped the business to reflect her belief and it has become a successful business model where the company has become a Fair-trade, organic business. A proportion of the profits go back into the community providing healthcare, education and leisure facilities for the workers and nearby villages. So, if you know your Home Quarter, you can bring aspects of it into your work and home to improve your life. Even if it takes time to realise your dream, you have made a start and by knowing, then adapting, you are on your way!

Read the descriptions of Tony, Fiona, Bridget and Carol. Which 'type' fits you best?

Imagine if at work you had teams with all the Quarters represented in them, the difference it would make to how customers are treated, planning, communicating, recruiting?

Can you name someone famous for being well-known or an expert in one Quarter. For example, perhaps the artist Picasso's Home Quarter was CREATE, Diana, Princess of Wales's Home Quarter was FEEL, Plato's was THINK and Doctor Martin Luther-King's was BELIEVE?

Think of four people who each represent one of the Quarters. They don't have to be someone famous now or in history. It could be someone you know personally. What qualities do they possess that you admire?

Think Name ______________________

Qualities ______________________

Feel Name ______________________

Qualities ______________________

Create Name ______________________

Qualities ______________________

Believe Name ______________________

Qualities ______________________

Denying Your Self

Whilst some people know their Home Quarter from an early age, many more people struggle to find their path. Others know theirs and then 'self-sabotage' and deny who they really are for all sorts of reasons (e.g. fear of failure, worries about leaving loved ones behind, fear of the unknown.) They also allow family, friends and mentors to talk them out of following their desire to do what is 'expected', 'right', 'worthy' all in the name of tradition or procrastination!

Think about someone in your life (perhaps a relative or family friend) who has rejected or been denied his/her Home Quarter.

How has this affected their life?

How would you be if you denied yourself or were refused the right to be who you truly are?

We will begin by getting you to know the Quarters through a relaxation exercise before you complete the 360 Quarter Profile to work out your Home Quarter. This will help you understand the quarters in your whole body as well as bring you to the centre of the 360 Circle where your journey begins.

Sit in a chair and place your feet firmly on the ground. Close your eyes and relax. Imagine you can feel your feet connected to the ground below. Be aware of the energy in your feet. Imagine it tingling and pulsating. See it like the green of new leaves, or think it or feel it moving up your legs and into your torso so you can feel it pulse against the base of your spine and inside your stomach. Keep the energy there. Feel its flow and power. This is CREATE.

Now allow the energy to move up your body to your chest and heart area. Keep the energy there for a couple of minutes. This colour is red like a rose. This is FEEL.

Move the energy up through your shoulders and neck into your head and feel the energy moving there. This colour is blue like a cloudless sky. Is it energising or relaxing or both? This is THINK.

Now, be aware of the other people in the space with you. (If you are alone, think of someone you love.) Let your energy flow through the top of your head into your body, then between your head, heart and gut and out to the people you love and to all the people you are yet to meet and know. They are bathed in gold dust. This is BELIEVE.

Which area inside the body did you feel most?
Where did the energy flow well?
How well did you connect with the other bodily Quarters?
What does your intuition tell you your Home Quarter is?

360 Quarter Profile

Now onto completing the profile. Here is a series of statements that will help you determine how 360 you are and which areas you could work on to improve your wisdom. Give yourself a rating on how you think you are doing right now by placing a mark in the relevant column. Be really honest with yourself about where you *really* are or you will skew your results. For example, if you don't enjoy learning new things and ideas, mark yourself *Poor*. If you recall quotes pretty well, then mark this *Good*. If you have first rate recall, then mark yourself *Excellent*.

When you have finished answering, transfer the answers from the Rating Sheet onto the profile sheet, so they are now running in numerical order, and then join the dots (see the example at the end).

When you have joined the dots, you will find it easier to see where you are in each quarter.

RATING SHEET

		Poor	Shaky	OK	Good	Excellent
12	I try to consider other people's perspectives to understand them better					
24	Ideas come to me easily					
37	I am inspired by vision and lead by example					
10	I am interested in personality testing					
35	I have a silent time every day					
20	I instinctively trust people I meet rather than them having to earn my trust					
32	I take joy in constructive and helpful actions, giving others what they need and like					
9	Things are only real if there is proof they exist					
16	I don't need other people's approval to feel good about myself					
31	I maintain a generous spirit towards others					
5	I am well qualified in what I do					
39	I believe in possibilities not just proof					
11	I enjoy talking to new people					
1	I'm receptive to new ideas and I enjoy learning					
27	I take breaks to daydream and use my imagination					
4	I often ask 'why' or 'what if?' questions					
17	I am open and authentic with people					
30	I enjoy variety in my food and am happy to try out new cuisine whenever I can					
36	Every morning, I set how I want my day to go and review it just before I go to sleep					
13	I don't judge others					
6	I like to think through a problem, considering a range of scenarios that could help solve it					
34	I know my core values and apply them in my life					
26	I love many different kinds of music					
18	When in conversation, I try to listen hard to what the other person is saying					
3	I recognise my patterns of thinking					
7	I see the connections between things					
14	I enjoy my own company					
22	I love making up stories and telling them					
2	I find it easy to remember quotes or phrases					
8	I set myself goals and plans for the future					
28	I doodle a lot and explain things by drawing pictures					
40	I'm prepared to go against the prevailing view, working against convention when necessary					
23	I am flexible and spontaneous					
19	I look for the meaning behind people's 'language' (verbal and non-verbal)					
29	I remember my dreams upon waking					
38	I live in the present, making the most of each day					
15	I spend time on my own each day relaxing and doing nothing					
21	I make things and/or grow things					
33	I love unconditionally					
25	I have a hobby or interest I enjoy					

360 QUARTER PROFILE SHEET

		Poor	Shaky	OK	Good	Excellent
1	I'm receptive to new ideas and I enjoy learning					
2	I find it easy to remember quotes or phrases					
3	I recognise my patterns of thinking					
4	I often ask 'why' or 'what if?' questions					
5	I am well qualified in what I do					
6	I like to think through a problem, considering a range of scenarios that could help solve it					
7	I see the connections between things					
8	I set myself goals and plans for the future					
9	Things are only real if there is proof they exist					
10	I am interested in personality testing					
11	I enjoy talking to new people					
12	I try to consider other people's perspectives to understand them better					
13	I don't judge others					
14	I enjoy my own company					
15	I spend time on my own each day relaxing and doing nothing					
16	I don't need other people's approval to feel good about myself					
17	I am open and authentic with people					
18	When in conversation, I try to listen hard to what the other person is saying					
19	I look for the meaning behind people's 'language' (verbal and non-verbal)					
20	I instinctively trust people I meet rather than them having to earn my trust					
21	I make things and/or grow things					
22	I love making up stories and telling them					
23	I am flexible and spontaneous					
24	Ideas come to me easily					
25	I have a hobby or interest I enjoy					
26	I love many different kinds of music.					
27	I take breaks to daydream and use my imagination					
28	I doodle a lot and explain things by drawing pictures					
29	I remember my dreams upon waking					
30	I enjoy variety in my food and am happy to try out new cuisine whenever I can					
31	I maintain a generous spirit towards others					
32	I take joy in constructive and helpful actions, giving others what they need and like					
33	I love unconditionally					
34	I know my core values and apply them in my life					
35	I have a silent time every day					
36	Every morning, I set how I want my day to go and review it just before I go to sleep					
37	I am inspired by vision and lead by example					
38	I live in the present, making the most of each day					
39	I believe in possibilities not just proof					
40	I'm prepared to go against the prevailing view, working against convention when necessary					

EXAMPLE OF JOINING THE DOTS	Poor	Shaky	OK	Good	Excellent
I'm receptive to new ideas and I enjoy learning.		*			
I recognise my patterns of thinking and try to change them whenever I can.			*		
I know my core values.					
I apply my values throughout my life.	*				
I like to think through a problem, considering a range of scenarios that could help solve it.	*				

Look to see what areas you are marking yourself Good or Excellent. Are they in one colour area, two or more or split over the whole range?

If you score strongly in one colour area, you have found your Home Quarter.

Blue = THINK, **Red** = FEEL, **Green** = CREATE, **Gold** = BELIEVE.

OK/Good/Excellent

Perhaps you have scored well in more than one colour? The great physicist Albert Einstein was known for combining his thinking skills and creative wisdom, so he probably had THINK and CREATE as Home Quarter's. You may be good or excellent in two or even three Quarters. It's difficult to be good in all four as most of us have a weaker Quarter.

Just imagine how much more amazing you will be if you can add a third and fourth quarter to your life!

If you have scored yourself OK or GOOD in all four Quarters, then you are an all-rounder! Check you have been truly honest about your capabilities and having shared your profile with others for some 360° feedback (see below), if the answers remain the same, then your challenge is to become excellent. It's like you see and hear the picture, but could turn up the sound and brightness and colour until they are vibrant and alive.

Shaky/Poor

Look to see where you are marking yourself Poor or Shaky. These areas represent your 'Away Quarters'. Focusing on improving these Quarters will help you become 360 wise. The exercises in this Guide will help you develop these quarters as well as the knowledge that there are people in your life who have your Away Quarters as their Home Quarter so that you could ask them for help. Alternatively, you could buy in help from professionals to advise and direct you so you can learn from them.

360 Team Quarter Profile

The 360 Wisdom profile has been adapted for use with groups at work and home. You and your colleagues and/or family will be able to complete individual profiles that can then be over-laid and mapped against each other. You will be able to see what Home Quarters each colleague possesses and where the 'void' is within the team. For example, you may find many of you are strong in THINK and feel with a little CREATE and no BELIEVE. The implications for your business can be explained and a remedial course of action planned. Please contact 360 Wisdom through the details given on the back cover of the 360 Wisdom Guide to discuss your requirements.

Share your completed 360 Quarter profile with a trusted family member, friend or colleague. Ask that person to look at your profile to give you some 360 feedback. What is their assessment of you? Where are the areas of difference between how you and they view you? What can you learn from this?

Verifying Your Home Quarter

If you aren't getting a clear result, here are more exercises to help you find your Home Quarter.

Sit somewhere quiet. Allow your body to feel the energy coming through your feet, up through your legs and slowly working its way up your torso, into your head, until your whole body is energised and relaxed.

Take yourself back gently to a time when everything was working really well for you and when you were at your best, connected, alive and awake. (If it takes a while, just trust yourself to get you there. Sometimes, you have to go back to adolescence or even earlier to childhood for that moment.) Recall the scene. Were you alone or with others? What was happening? Really notice the detail, the colours, the sounds and smells. What was your part in this? How did you feel and think? What made it so special?

Spend some time writing down your recollections. Get as detailed and as accurate a picture as you can. If you enjoy illustrating, feel free to draw or add colours to the picture to evoke the mood and emotions of that time.

Put aside your recollections for a few minutes. Stretch your legs, have a drink or food, or take a walk outdoors.

Return to your recollection. Are there clear links to any of the Quarters? Were you doing something creative or making a decision based on options and evidence? Did you put someone else's concerns before your own or were you doing something that befitted the environment? Were you just 'being' with nature?

If it helps, underline key things in the 360 colours below.

Blue = THINK, **Red** = FEEL, **Green** = CREATE, **Gold** = BELIEVE.

We are going to create a 360 Wisdom timeline. Find as big a piece of paper as you can and draw a horizontal line across it. On the left side write 0 and on the far right side, your current age, for example, here's a time-line for Bridget:

Bridget

0 **66**

Now, mark off on the horizontal line all the **key things** that have happened in your life so far. Think carefully about this. Sometimes, small things make a big impact. Bridget has a fear of heights but was not sure why until she completed her time-line. When she was eight, her family came to England for a holiday and visited Cornwall. Her parents took her to Tintagel. In those days, the descent to the ancient site was down narrow steps near the cliff edge. Bridget held her mother's hand believing she would be protected. But her mother was terrified when she saw the drop and clung onto her daughter for dear life. It meant nothing at the time but when she remembered the incident Bridget realised when her fear had started. She also recalled that she wasn't afraid herself but her memory had absorbed her mother's fear as if it were her own. Knowing this now makes it easier to overcome something she can no longer own.

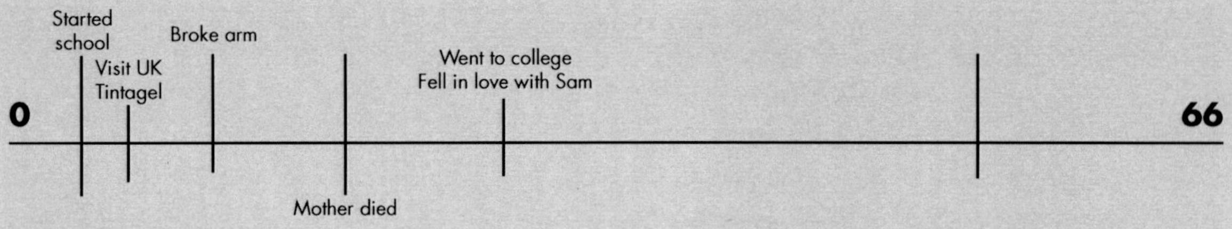

Look carefully through your completed time-line and consider it from a 360 perspective. How much of your life has been like Tony's for example? Is there more THINK or FEEL, CREATE or BELIEVE or is it a mixture of some and less of others?

How would your partner describe you? (If you don't have one at present, use your best friend or somebody else who knows you well and whose opinion you value). Using any colour (but not red), pick a colour and write all the words that come to mind.

How would your parent/s or guardian/s describe you? In another colour, write down all the words that come to mind.

How would your sibling/s describe you? In another colour, write down all that comes to mind.

How would your boss and/or work colleagues describe you? In another colour, write down all the words that come to mind.

Finally, write down in another colour all the words you'd use to describe yourself.

Notice key words that are common to most of the perspectives used and ring them in red. You should come up with a list of key descriptive words or 'red flags' that are common to all descriptions. Now, assess these against the 360 Wisdom model. Do you see you are more THINK or BELIEVE, CREATE OR FEEL?

Now you should have an understanding about your Home Quarter. You should also be aware of the Quarters you can develop (your AWAY Quarters).

Section Two: The Ranges

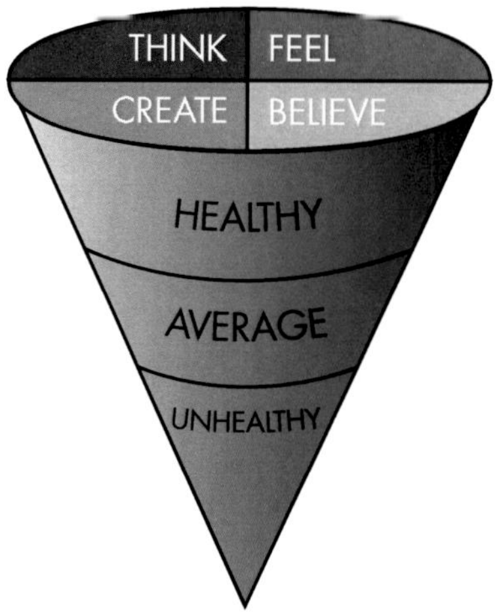

There are Three 'Ranges': *Healthy, Average* and *Unhealthy*

The 360 Quarter Profile can be mapped to these Ranges as follows

Excellent/Good	= Healthy	e.g. fit, well, strong, vigorous.
OK	= Average	e.g. normal, regular, run-of-the-mill.
Shaky/Poor	= Unhealthy	e.g. damaged, toxic, harmful.

Describe in one word only a) how you feel on a good/healthy day, b) an OK/ average day and c) a poor/unhealthy day.

Average Range

Most people live in the Average Range where the Home Profile is working 'OK'.

In my workshops, I find people describe an 'Average day' as 'OK', 'drifting', 'ordinary', 'nothing', 'bland', 'boring'. Did you do something similar? If so, this is your default position. It's sad that most people live their lives away feeling dull and bored rather than 'energised', 'joyous', 'alive', 'at peace' (the descriptions I get for 'Good days'.) Yet, these days form only a small part of most people's lives. We should aim for all our days to be good or excellent!

What causes us to shift from the Average 'default' Range? Something happens that I like to call 'crisis' or 'vision'.) When you have vision, everything seems to fall into place. In a crisis you feel out of control of your life.

Usually, the crisis is caused by the outer world affecting you. The vision comes from your inside and gets projected out into the world. Sadly, due to the power and pressure of the outside world, we tend to have more crises to deal with. This only changes when you recognise where you are and dig yourself out of the situation (usually) by breaking old habits and patterns to try something new. Whilst some people call this growing and learning, my view is 'why put yourself through all that angst and upset if you can avoid it in the first place?'

Sometimes, people are born, grow and live without realising there's a better state of being. They are in effect asleep.

"Spirituality means waking up. Most people, even though they don't know it, are asleep. They're born asleep, they live asleep, they marry in their sleep, they breed children in their sleep, they die in their sleep without ever waking up. They never understand the loveliness and the beauty of this thing that we call human existence." [2]

360 Wisdom has been designed to wake you up and keep you awake to be at one with the world, exploring and enjoying it and adding value to it.

Unhealthy Range

Sadly, there are many people who fall from the Healthy or Average Range state to the Unhealthy level. There are many reasons why this can happen. If I had to summarise, I would say this is due to a lack of confidence and sometimes fear which allows others to run our lives. Some people simply just don't know what to do so they can't or don't make choices.

Once they drop into this Range they are further and further away from balance, feeling more and more wobbly until in extreme cases, they become delusional, violent towards themselves and others, out of touch and out of control.

I believe that each Quarter has a specific relationship to certain illnesses and addictions which become apparent at the lower end of the Unhealthy Range. We will touch on this a little in each of the four Quarters. The link between the Ranges and wellness will be explored further in separate publications.

Sometimes, you can be functioning in the Unhealthy Range, yet still produce. It is, however, not possible to do this for long without seriously affecting your health and well-being. The composer Mozart created the most exquisite music from the Unhealthy Range in CREATE. This led to an impoverished emotional and material life. So, for most of you, living to extremes in your Home Quarter isn't a good thing!

At its extreme end, overuse or dependency on external stimuli, e.g., drugs, alcohol, sex etc, can be an indication of living in the lower regions of the Unhealthy Range as can a range of psychosis and pathological behaviours. Here, therapies and other medical interventions will be required. 360 Wisdom does not provide this professional support but it can help support people as their health recovers and is designed to help the shaky move along the Average Range and up into the Healthy Range.

Healthy Range

We all get glimpses of the Healthy Range, sometimes for a few seconds or even days. The experience is one of feeling expansive, generous and joyful. It is as if you no longer feel confined in your body; that you are connected to everyone and everything. When healthy, you are in the state known as 'flow'. It's like a natural high an athlete feels when s/he has won a race. It's the exhilaration you get when you have climbed a mountain or seen a wonderful view. It's like the day where everything goes right and you have a 'knowing' that all is well and you can do no wrong. It has been written about by mystics for centuries and some have called it the state of enlightenment or bliss. You don't have to wait to go to heaven or Nirvana or any other after-life to be in the Healthy Range. You can live it NOW. It is human being. *The trick is to know where you are and shift towards the centre of the 360 Wisdom Circle.*

KEY

1	Outer circle	Unhealthy
2	Second circle	Average
3	Inner circle	Healthy

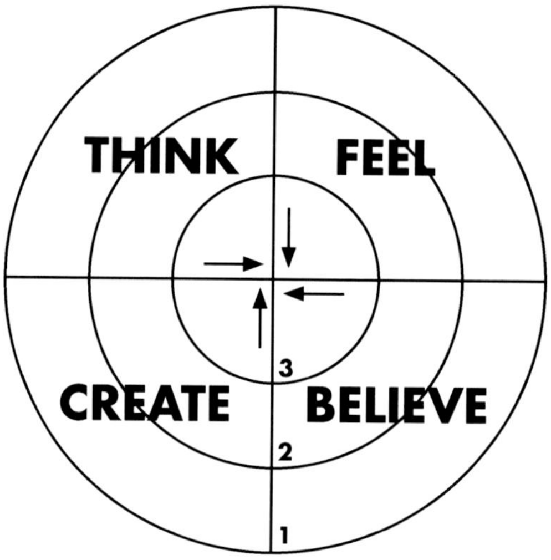

The starting point to get you there is to recognise what Range you are operating in your Home Quarter (*Unhealthy, Average* or *Healthy*).

Look at the above diagram and consider what Range you fall in for each Quarter. For example, you may decide you fall into 2 Average in THINK, 3 Unhealthy in FEEL and so on. Mark the curved lines in a coloured pen. Unless you are Healthy in all four Quarters, it's likely your final diagram will look like a wobbly, flat tyre!

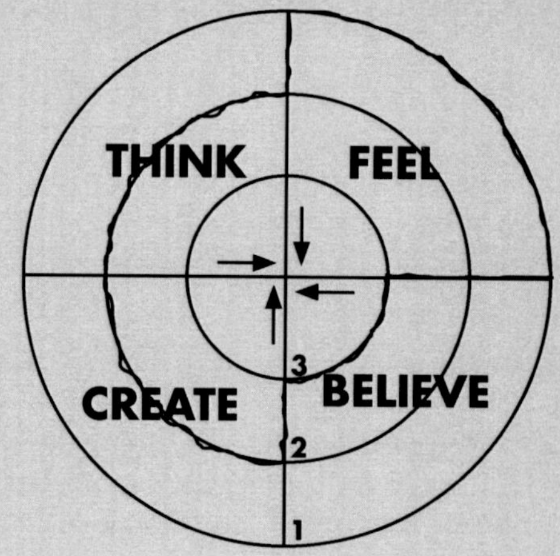

Although you can jump in and out of the Ranges throughout your life as you react to situations and people, you will gradually improve them to healthy. This diagram is designed to remind you of your starting point!

You will see in THINK (below) examples of healthy, average and unhealthy thinking and then in FEEL, CREATE and BELIEVE. Remember that most people live in their Home Quarter Average Range, dropping into Unhealthy according to the '*slings and arrows of outrageous fortune.*' [3] At this point in the Guide, the aim is to keep you from dropping out of Average Range by making you aware of the stages of decline through *Red Flagging*.

Later, when you have worked through THINK, FEEL, CREATE, BELIEVE, you stand on the DIAMOND (page 65). The Diamond is the centre-point where the four Quarters are aligned, with each other and on the Healthy Ranges for each of the Quarters as well. This makes you centred, grounded and balanced simultaneously. It is akin to balancing on the knife-edge of the moment.

By the time you arrive at the Diamond, you will have learned techniques to keep you from 'dropping out' and 'falling through' and if you do on occasion fall out and through, you will know how to climb back up when you are ready and you will bounce back quicker.

The Shadow Effect

When you are a *human being*, just reflecting and being in the quiet, you are close to falling from that state of grace which is aligned and balanced. You are small steps away from the Unhealthy Range. Knowing that the shadows lurk beneath the surface pulling you back into *human doing*, should be enough to keep you aware and alert. There's some fantastic work on the Shadow Effect by Debbie Ford[4] if you want to learn more about this.

So, 360 Wisdom people do everything to develop the positive aspects of their Home Quarters and Healthy Ranges when they have this cracked, they do the same with their Away Quarters.

Then the song title 'Home on the Range' will make perfect sense!

Write down as many examples as you can for healthy, average and unhealthy THINKing. Then do the same for FEEL, CREATE and BELIEVE. (Examples are given on page 27 for THINK, page 35 for FEEL, page 45 for CREATE and page 53 for BELIEVE.)

Examples of these Range 'States' for each Quarter are given on pages 27, 35, 45, 53.

The Range Scales

Questions and Actions

Do you consider you exist in the healthy, average or unhealthy range in your Home Quarter?

Use these Range Scales to guide you.

- Scale One 1-3 = Unhealthy
- Scale Two 4-7 = Average
- Scale Three 8-10 = Healthy

If you have scored yourself at Scale One, ask yourself the following and if helpful, write your thoughts in the Range Scales notes section at the back of this Guide.

- What are you going to do about this?
- What are you denying in yourself or not facing up to?

If you seem stuck in the Unhealthy, should you consider the possibility of getting some outside help? Coaching, therapy or medical advice may be required here.

If you have scored yourself at Scale Two, how can you change your patterns of THINK, FEEL, CREATE, BELIEVE to improve to Scale Three? Are you really completing the exercises in this Guide to the fullest extent of your ability? What actions could you put in place to take you into the Healthy Range?

If you have scored yourself at Scale Three, appreciate where you have got to. What do you do on a regular basis that keeps you in the Healthy Range Scale? Be aware of the Shadow Effect lurking. Look back on your past on your time-line once more. Can you see which past events and episodes were in the Healthy, Average and Unhealthy Ranges? Can you see patterns emerging? What did you do to move out of those situations? Are these mechanisms you can employ over and over again to keep you Healthy?

Consider 10 people who play a major part in your life right now e.g. your partner, family members, close friends, acquaintances, work colleagues and rate them on the Range Scale. Give them a score.

Who have you have scored at Scale One, Scale Two, Scale Three?

Can you offer help and support to those at Scale One if you are a higher Scale? If you are at Scale One yourself, could you help each other ? Are they helping or holding you down? Are these the best people to be spending time with? Are they damaging to you right now?

Who did you score at Scale Two or Three? Could you work with someone you have identified on a higher scale to you to improve your Range ?

Who did you score at Scale Three? If you are Scale Two, what lifestyle are they leading to be Healthy? What can you learn from them? Find out how they do it and copy what they do.

If you scored yourself at Scale Three and did the same for some of your group, you will already understand it's your responsibility to help others on lower Ranges. What are you doing together to help your loves ones and people you can influence?

We now turn to an in-depth look at the profiles for each of the four Quarters in order to improve your proficiency in each one to bring yourself back into balance.

Section Three: THINK

"Not that he is great who can alter matter, but he who can alter my state of mind."
(Ralph Emerson)

- Thinking for yourself and recognising your thinking patterns and where they come from. Using logic and rationale to make decisions. **THINK**.

Tony the Thinker
When Tony was twenty three, he was waiting for a train home when a beautiful woman Jane, sat next to him and started up a conversation. Tony the THINKER's heart was touched. He felt emotionally attracted and totally connected to this stranger. It was as if cupid's arrow had hit his heart dead centre. He wasn't used to feeling this way.

When Jane invited him to dinner the next evening, he accepted without hesitation. He felt she could be his soul mate and big love. Jane gave him her address on a piece of paper; 137 Coldharbour Lane. At the appointed time, Tony walked along the lane reading the ascending door numbers. They stopped at 133 and round the corner, began again at 17. Tony walked up and down several times, confused at first and then thinking more and more that he'd been set up. Jane (probably not her real name) had seen him for a patsy. He returned home angry, his heart hardened.

Thirty years later, Tony found himself once more on Coldharbour Lane, but this time he approached it from the opposite end in his car. He was reminded of 'Jane'. On occasion, he mourned for her as he'd never connected with another woman in the same way since. As his car turned the same bend, he saw a fork in the road he'd not noticed before and to his horror, the numbers picked up 135, 137, 139.

Jane, he surmised, had waited for him all night with a congealing meal, thinking he was a rat for not showing up.

If only he'd thought differently and not assumed the road forked one way not two. If he'd not jumped to his usual conclusions, changed his thinking and considered the possibility there was another solution, who knows what would have happened and how different his life would be?

We live in the age of the thinker, where logic and deductive reasoning reigns. Some argue this attention to thinking comes from the fact that the part of the brain that does this (the cerebral cortex in the frontal lobe) in evolutionary terms is the most recent. It has brought great technological advancement and the structures and systems we enjoy today.

Thinking is vital in many ways. You need to know options and choices to make sound decisions. You need to think to manage day to day activities, to solve problems and plan.

What Influences Your THINKing?

Each person has an internal 'map of reality' formed by unique experiences from birth. No two people are the same because we all live different lives.

Most 'maps' are 'charted' quite early on in life. Human behaviourist, Dr. Morris Massey[5] suggests these three main 'Formation Periods' impacting a person's view of external reality:

1. **The Imprint Period.** This is information absorbed up to the age of seven. The major influences here are parents/guardians, siblings and close relatives.
2. **The Modelling Period.** This is where the influence of school, (teachers and friends), religion, clubs and social activities develop from eight to thirteen.
3. **The Socialisation Period** from thirteen to twenty-one may involve first love, further/higher education or work, volunteering, networking.

Dr Massey believed these Periods form your thinking and the way you think is set by your early twenties. You rarely change this 'mind-set'. It takes a lot to think outside this box, to form new thinking patterns. The trick with THINK is to be aware of these patterns and to check yourself before you act whether the pattern should be repeated or replaced.

The more startling thing to consider is this: how much of your thinking belongs to you, or are many of your thoughts 'externally imprinted' via your parents, teachers, friends and society?

Think about each of the three Formation Periods. Can you remember key incidents for example from seven to fourteen that will have expanded or altered your map? (Your time-line may be a useful 'memory-jogger.')

Write them down and then think about how much they may have influenced how you view things.

- Where do you still think like a seven year old in some important areas of your life?!
- Could you do something to change that to be the age you are now?

Think about a problem you have at work or home. Can you see if you have got into 'thinking loop' where you are repeating the same thinking patterns? What would happen if you think differently to do things differently to make a difference?

What We Perceive

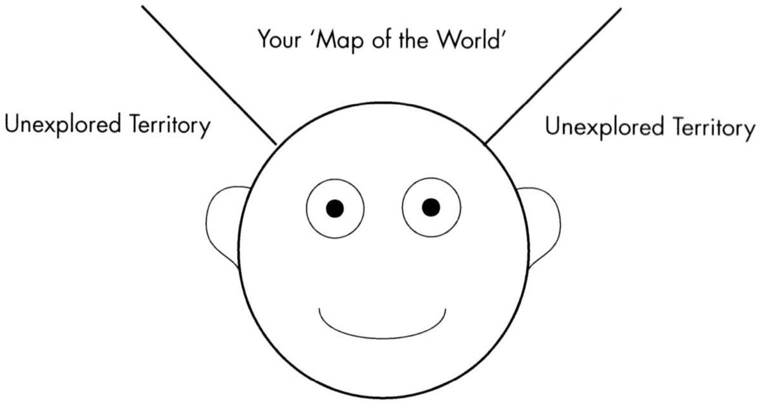

There are literally millions of bits of information swirling around us each second. Our senses can only absorb and process a small percentage of them, so we select what is familiar. When everyone believed the world was flat, think how hard it was to convince people it might be round.

Perhaps we are like the 'flat-earthers'; discrediting things that do not fit our current map of the world. Yet, there are many things still to be discovered that we cannot explain right now. We need to stay open minded and curious for there are many things and experiences yet to be discovered that our minds can barely comprehend at this stage in our evolution.

Look directly ahead at an object in front of you and focus on it. Without moving your eyes from the object, become aware of what lies on either side of it, then expand it a little more. Keep doing this until you reach the limits of your vision (you may surprise yourself and feel like you can see round the back of your head!) Then bring your attention and focus back to the object before you and repeat.

There is a lot you haven't been noticing. Try going into expanded vision when you next go walking and see what it does to your awareness. Make some notes.

The 'familiar' as defined by Massey's Periods, affects our language, our values, the way we view time, our beliefs, attitudes and communication. For example, the Inuit have far more words for snow than the English. The Chinese experience time as circular. In the West, we tend to view it as linear. What we are used to affects how we THINK.

If, for example, I practice a religion, my brain will 'search' for meaning and select from the millions of bits of information for I will ignore or bypass anything that doesn't fit these views. If my 'religion' is money, I will search for ways of making, saving and investing it.

For example, Fiona's mother THINKS that her country has been ruined by all the immigrants that have 'swamped' it. She THINKS they have jumped the queue for benefits and do very little work in return. Fiona thought the same as she grew up. To justify these thoughts, mother and daughter self-selected information in the newspapers and on television and ignored viewpoints and data that told a different story. When Fiona began training for social work, she met refugees whose lives were under threat because they'd championed freedom of speech in a dictatorship. She witnessed skilled economic migrants working hard in jobs her countrymen and women were less qualified or inclined to do. Fiona began to read different newspapers to her parents and watch more investigative television programmes on the subject. Over time, her thinking changed, broadened by her experiences. Today, Fiona recognises many migrants add to the economic wealth and productivity of the country and sees a 'diversity advantage' that has cultural, social and economic value. She is far less judgmental in her views on this topic. Fiona has learned to explore the territory outside of her Imprint Period to form her own thinking on this subject.

Absorbing Others' Maps

Your attitude towards a person or thing can be formed by taking others' maps into your own. When it's positive, it can be a great learning opportunity.

There's a whole world out there that you will never be able to explore in a lifetime, so others' experiences can help you fill the gaps. This is the beauty of interacting with people from different backgrounds, races, religions and cultures.

But be mindful of the maps you are 'taking in' and their impact. Maps can be so powerful, they can influence whole civilisations as well as the individual. A country or religion can think another harmful and pass this thinking onto their offspring. The negative maps can be passed on for generations. It's very difficult to stop the thinking patterns and reflect on the positive aspects, the common ground and the learning opportunities. As Alfred Korzybski[6] once said: *'The map is not the territory!'*

Shift Past Thinking

Spend some time reflecting on how you have changed your thinking in the past to see if there are useful lessons you have learned and can take with you on your journey.

Recall one example of how you came to think differently about something. How did it happen and why?

Do you have a negative example like Fiona's, where she took a long time to realise her views on immigration were not her own but her mother's? Could you expand your map on this subject? Here's some ways you can do this.

Sit with an older person and ask them their experiences about their childhood and key events in their life.

Network with people from different cultures, work backgrounds and interests. This will put you in touch with people who are culturally different to you, have different values and beliefs about life and a fantastic history to learn about, thus expanding your world map further.

Go to a meeting or experience something you think you might not like much or read an article or a book that puts the alternative view to your own. Suspend your judgment, letting yourself go with the flow.

If you want to get things done, you may need to compromise or at least understand the issue from the perspective of 'the Other'. This is the individual or group outside of your usual networks who may have a different or opposing view, feeling, idea or belief to your own. To try to find a 'balanced view' where both parties may be able to find a common map to work from, it helps to put yourself into the perspective of others.

As the predominant model in the world is rational, most of us would initially put THINK down as Home Quarter. So, to do the other Quarters justice, we need to tone it down our THINKing to reveal the truth beneath and increase the power of CREATE, FEEL, BELIEVE, so that there's some equilibrium.

THINKing Now

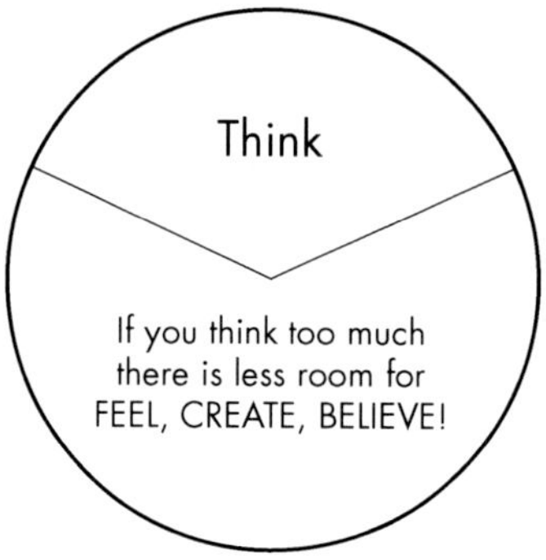

If your profile and the other exercises reveal your Home Quarter is THINK, do you recognise elements of the Tony the Thinker in your behaviour and outlook on life?

Who are the Thinkers in your personal and work life? What would it be like to just have a group of thinkers in a room?

Consider your interactions with Thinkers. What could you do to get better results from your relationship with them?

How much THINKing are you doing to the exclusion of the other Quarters?

The likelihood of THINKing too much is that it becomes Unhealthy and takes you closer to the 'Shadow Effect. The same applies if you FEEL, CREATE or BELIEVE too much. You lose your balance within your Home Quarter and live in a smaller portion of your Away Quarters.

Thinking Ranges

Here's some examples of the Ranges for THINK. They are to help you understand when your quality of THINKing declines.

Healthy Thinking

- The mind is quiet and clear.
- Healthy thinkers speak with a conviction and clarity that takes others with them.
- They are good at decision-making, having weighed up the options before making a choice.
- They keep calm in a crisis whilst others are losing their heads.
- They make good strategists if they focus on the bigger picture.
- Their positive mind anticipates success, happiness and successful outcomes to every situation.
- They recognise and are content with the strengths and weaknesses caused by these patterns.

Average Thinking

- They are fair, considered and trustworthy in their judgment.
- They know how the ingredients went into their thinking 'patterns'.
- When they say 'I know this', they switch down.
- They are less open to possibilities and unconventional routes.
- They tend not to see things from others' perspectives.
- They don't reveal their feelings and dislike others showing theirs.
- They are not necessarily practical. They can read an instruction manual but not put the thing together.
- They can be indecisive when things aren't going to plan.

Unhealthy Thinking

- They get fixated and obsessive about a past event, mulling it over and over in their minds.
- They speak their mind and this can be hurtful and offensive to others.
- They acquire more and more knowledge without understanding its meaning.
- They have a tendency to focus on too much detail and this can cause them worry and stress.
- They close down their feelings and beliefs.
- They become locked in by their thoughts and can't see a way out.
- The extreme of THINK is burnout and 'losing one's mind'.
- Can lead to taking one's life.

Danger Signal

As soon as Thinkers say to themselves, "We know this", they switch off and close down to new possibilities. They also move into their head and accumulate more knowledge and information without understanding it. When a Thinker quotes at you and tries to beat you down with a raft of information, they have ceased to understand, to know.

How to Make a Thinker Happy

- Give them a puzzle to solve.
- Get them to classify or prioritise something.

They prefer to be given things in written form and time to consider the implications. Never give a thinker an impromptu presentation!

You will make an impact with them if you stay calm and focused and present a clear argument. Thinkers don't 'get' emotional blackmail or histrionics.

Steps to Improve Your Quality of THINKing

The ideas here will help you move up the Ranges as well.

1. Quieten the Mind

Try to spend ten minutes every morning and evening somewhere quiet. Sit in a position you find comfortable and go through the relaxation technique in Exercise One on page 11. If thoughts come in your mind, let them go by noting them as if you are just observing them coming from the outside like a small imaginary insect that you gently bat away. After a little practice, your thoughts will become less and less and you will find your mind becomes quiet and still.

During the day, if you find your thoughts are filling your mind to the point you can't THINK straight, a technique I use based on the Buddhist's mindful walking can be helpful.

Stand and cup your hands resting them on your stomach. Imagine you are wearing the old-fashioned deep-sea diver's boots or heavy ski boots so you are aware of your feet being anchored to the ground. Walk slowly (in a straight line or circle, it doesn't matter) lifting your feet and being aware of each step as you leave the earth and gently plant it back down in a slow step. Look straight ahead at the scene around you as if you are a camera taking in the scene without thought or pre-conceived ideas. (If you are blind or partially sighted, use your ears like a tape recorder and your skin like a barometer, sensing the changes of air, heat, cold on your skin.) After a while, your mind will calm down and empty its thoughts and you will feel peaceful and alert.

2. Shift the Mindset

Ronnie Lessem[7] wrote a paper entitles 'Life Phases'. There are seven main stages of life in his theory:

17-22	Early adult transition.	This is about leaving adolescence behind and stepping into the adult world.
22-28	The novice phase.	Forming your 'dream' for what you want to be and finding a mentor to guide you through to turn this into an occupation.
28-32	Age 30 transition.	Beginning to work on your character flaws.
32-40	The settling down phase.	Establishing a niche in society, anchoring life and work more fully, advancing and progressing.
40-45	The mid-life transition.	Reappraisal of the early adult ladder. Understanding basic meanings of success and failure. Engaging with the 'inner self'.
45-52	The mid-life phase of renewal.	Integrating the outer/inner self and polarities of young/old, masculine/feminine, destruction/creation, attachment/separateness.
52+	The legacy phase.	What you pass onto future generations. Your ultimate vision leading to profound creativity.

As we age, we don't necessarily move onto the next phase. We can become 'stuck' and never move on. (I know men and women who are still in the Adolescent phase, acting out as if they were still teenagers!) Lessem says the way to move to the next stage is to 'Die a little'. You do this by letting go or giving up on something to create the space to take on the new. In other words, you let go of a part of your map to take on the new territory, perhaps with the spirit of the pioneers of old! Be aware of how you die a little every day!

3. THINK a Healthy Future

The key is to be aware of old THINKING patterns, and to decide which ones to keep or discard as you move forward.

Continue to be curious, to expand your THINKing map.

Balance your THINKing by developing your Away Quarters.

What Influences Feeling?

Feelings are triggered in you by physical sensations from the outside world received through the senses, giving an emotional response. For example, smelling a flower may make you feel relaxed, or you may feel tender towards someone when they hug you.

Feelings can also be triggered in the brain by past memories and future events. For example, feeling excited about your birthday as the last one was such fun! Past negative experiences like being bullied at school can cause emotional anxiety and fear in someone. Triggers include finding yourself in a similar environment to one in the past, similar words used, behaviour that you associate with.

One of the challenges about the FEEL Quarter is that what one person feels through internalising external influences, will be very different to another. Someone can cut their finger and feel great pain, making them cry or another can hardly feel anything at all.

Despite these differences in the sensitivity and severity of individual feelings, you try to collectively categorise them into a 'continuum' of feelings. Most people would say 'love' is a positive feeling and 'hate' a negative one and there are a whole range of feelings in between. To make it even more complex, too much love can be negative as channelling hate (for example, you may hate businesses that pollute the environment) into positive outcomes (for example, become active in environmental charities that lobby to cut emissions). But generally, you decide individually and collectively that there are good and bad feelings even if your interpretation of them differs.

We can also find it hard to interpret how others are feeling. When one person feels love towards another, it might be reciprocated, but not to the same degree.

We can also over-indulge in feelings. Imagine the romantic heroine from novels and films walking the fields full of melancholy feelings due to unrequited love. She revels in the extreme feelings she experiences to the point where she *becomes* those emotions and gets held in a space and time by them.

Cultures have different attitudes to feelings and they can change over time.

Tony was taught at school and by his parents to display a 'stiff upper lip', to not show his emotions in public. Brenda's childhood on the tea plantation was filled with singing, dancing, fun and happiness with the workers and people in the local villages.

Society can tell you to hide or show your feelings. It determines some are 'good' (joy), or 'bad' (e.g. anger). This is not true. Sometimes, it's good to feel angry so you can let go and move on quickly. We can learn a lot from these feelings. But, sometimes, you don't show how you feel to avoid causing bad feelings in others or you believe it's not socially appropriate to express them or to take time to analyse the feelings and how best to repond.

If you keep on hiding your feelings like this, over time, you don't even realise you are doing it. You push your feelings so deep inside, they are hidden from your awareness, only for them to pop out later on and surprise you.

The above examples show us that as human beings, feelings are the *experiential* of anger as well as happiness. They are *basic sensations* (pleasure and pain) and *driven states* e.g. hunger and thirst.

You are going to create a Feelings Spectrum to help you focus on the feelings you live with most of the time. Draw a line across a piece of paper. Write down as many feelings as you can and group them across the line from positive at the one end to negative at the other. Now mark off the sorts of feelings you exhibit on a day to day basis. (This exercise will also help you work out where you are on the FEEL Range when you look at them on page 35). Do you feel joy and contentment most days, or is it all about being cross, resentful and angry?

You could also do this exercise with your partner, friend or colleague. By looking at both Feelings Spectrums, you will see where they place their feelings in relation to yours and what state they are in most of the time.

Check whether you have misinterpreted their general state of feeling and whether they have with you. Do you need to say more how you are feeling?

How Feelings Originated

If the cerebral cortex was considered to be the seat of reason, the limbic system in the cerebellum was believed to be the home of emotions. The limbic is the oldest part of the brain in evolutionary terms and is responsible for regulating all our basic functions e.g. breathing, body temperature.

Historically, there has been confusion about where feelings come from in a person. William James[8] believed they come from stimuli outside and inside the body, get recognised in the brain and which jogs our memories and imagination and then we make up a story to explain them. Walter Cannon[8] thought the opposite - that they originated in the head and trickled down through the body. The debate between these two opposing views continued for many years right up until the 1980's where the view taken was it was both simultaneously.

More recently, it's been found that memories are not only stored in the brain but are present in a psychosomatic network in the body and these memories are transferred across into new cells. Neuroscientist Candace B. Pert[8] has made a significant contribution in field. So, the memory of feelings (good and bad) can potentially be stored in parts of the body. If we don't deal with those feelings and instead bury them, this could build and build into a big storehouse of trouble, resulting in all kinds of illnesses (some of them being terminal in extreme cases).

When the cell dies, (our bodies make new cells all of the time and in the course of a year, most of our cells are completely replenished), the memory does not die with it. Instead, it transfers into the new replicated cell. This can explain how difficult it is to give up addictions (food, alcohol, drugs, sex). A cigarette smoker for example, may give up the physical act of smoking, but the pleasure given from the release of a range of stimulating chemicals like nicotine gets transferred into the new cells memory to survive long after the chemical has worked its way out. This is why years after, when someone lights up a cigarette near you, the craving returns. This also applies to intolerances. Bridget can't drink orange juice. It makes her feel sick. This is because when she was ten she was drinking a glass of orange when her father came to tell her, her mother had been killed in a car crash. Whatever your drug of choice e.g. nicotine, food, alcohol, drugs, the same applies.

This means when we become addicted to something, it takes us into the Average or Unhealthy Range and a significant shift in thinking and feeling will be required to combat it.

The implications are quite stark in terms of how to manage your feelings in this context. A 'steady as you go' approach of curbing or limiting feelings and addictions will help with the effects but not necessarily solve the cause. You have to shift into a new feelings space just as you have done with the mind in THINK.

For centuries, Buddhists have recognised the term 'cause and effect'. Every experience is triggered by a previous one which gets conjured up as an 'imprint' when the present experience is taking place. Buddhism believes this can occur across lifetimes.

Geshe Michael Roach(9) says "*No experience of any kind ever happens unless there is a previous imprint that causes it, it is equally true that – once an imprint is planted – it must lead to an experience. Imprints are never wasted; they always have an effect, they always cause us to perceive something.*"

Now scientists like Candace B. Pert suggest we have a body-mind, it feels right to say that feelings can be transferred in this way. These 'emotional imprints' work the same as mental imprints. Geshe Michael Roach suggests: "*We just have to figure out which imprint it is that we can plant in our minds to see, later on....and this depends primarily on maintaining certain states of mind, maintaining certain standards of behaviour, and knowing how to call on the power of what we call an 'act of truth'* ".

So, the trick is to recognise negative feelings and addictions, know they are stored in the 'body' memory and at the very least, this memory goes beyond the life of a cell across into new ones. This breaks into the cycle of triggering off the old set of feelings every time a certain experience or event takes place.

To do this, know how you are feeling, experience your feelings as they occur and then let them go. Let your mind play a role here in deciding this and how you are going to handle your emotions the next time a similar situation or stimulus happens.

How Are You Feeling?

If you've answered: 'I feel happy/sad/confused/', you are expressing yourself without any barriers.

If you've answered: 'I am feeling happy'/sad/confused, you are one step away from feeling your feelings. You have created a barrier, (the 'am feeling' is the self disassociated by one step. You are hiding your feelings a little!).

- How often do you express your feelings directly or indirectly? What impact could that have on you over time?
- What feelings do you hide and why?
- What feelings do you dislike or find extreme in others?
- Where have you over-indulged your feelings in the past and 'become them'?
- Are you still doing this now with some feelings? Can you recall when or why this happened?

If you have scored FEEL as your Home Quarter, you will primarily run your inner and outer worlds from an emotional perspective. How much do you recognise elements of Fiona the FEELer in your behaviour and outlook on life?

Who are the 'FEELers' in your personal and work life? What would it be like to just have a group of FEELers in a room?

Consider your interactions with FEELers. What could you do to get better results from your relationship with them?

How much FEELing are you doing to the exclusion of the other Quarters?

FEEL Ranges

Here are some examples of the FEEL ranges. They will act as your guide to where you are on the FEEL Range.

Healthy Feeling

- Healthy FEELERS are compassionate, caring and understanding of others needs.
- They are great fun to be around, possessing a great sense of humour that's self-deprecating.
- They are extrovert, spontaneous and live in the present.
- They are modest, charitable, gentle and benevolent.
- People say they are 'full of good heart', always on hand to help another.
- They give comfort in a crisis.
- Their world is full of hope and promise.

Average Feeling

- They are sensitive to others, aware of their own feelings.
- They are honest about their feelings.
- They are aware of what triggers their feelings and their patterns.
- They start to tell others how they should be feeling.
- They start people pleasing, putting others feelings before their own.
- They start to internalise their feelings.
- They become moody, irritable and self-absorbed.

Unhealthy Feeling

- They are desperate for love and 'strokes' from anyone. This can lead to extremes e.g. promiscuity.
- They close down their feelings and withdraw.
- They become locked in by their feelings and can't see a way out of their fantasy world.
- This can lead to hypochondria, depression, nervous breakdown and possibly suicide.

Danger Signal

As soon as a FEELer starts telling others what they are feeling or should be feeling in a situation, it's a sign they are losing touch with their own feelings. This could herald the beginning of passing into the extremes of the feeling continuum and the beginnings of self-introspection. When a FEELer goes 'high, low' or withdrawn, they have moved from the Healthy and Average feeling Ranges.

What feelings do you associate with each of the Quarters e.g. what would someone with a THINK Home Quarter feel?

Consider your interactions with each from the perspective of your Home Quarter FEEL.

What could you do to bring about positive feelings in others by changing your behaviour? Do you need to FEEL more or less? How would it benefit you if you did?

What would it be like to just have a group of feelers in a room?

FEEL Now

Steps to Stop Negative FEELings

It's a scary feeling to think (or a scary thought to feel...) that negative feelings get stored until they cause damage to the body and these stay in the body memory long after the original 'body' has died (i.e. our cells have reproduced.) Yet most people don't even realise what their feelings are. Sometimes, you can judge your feelings to be negative because society has told you it's wrong to feel this way. For example, some cultures suggest it's inappropriate to be jealous of someone's success. If you feel jealous, you may have to deny it, mask it or even pretend the feeling doesn't exist.

Look back to the exercise you did in the Ranges for how you are on a good, average and bad day (page 18).

It's worrying to note that the vast majority of us spend most of our days with negative feelings. (My groups tell me most of their days are average or bad with only a few good days.)

Can anything be done to turn this negative tide? Thankfully, the answer is *yes*.

Just as in THINK, the trick is to recognise how you are feeling. If they are negative feelings, be aware of them, experience them, understand why you have them and let them go. There are some examples and exercises below and on the next page to help you do this.

Move to FEELing positive. Find things that make you feel good about yourself, that make you happy. Take pleasure in life. Be joyous.

Get Into Your Body

Get back in touch with your body. Take a regular massage. Have an aromatherapy session. (Smell is one of our most primitive senses and it takes a quicker, unfiltered route from body to mind consciousness because the nose is very near to the amalgdala (that is a nodal point routing incoming sensory information into the higher centres of association in the cerebral cortex). Similarly, visit a sensory garden and gently touch the plants and smell their perfume.

'My Heart Touch.'

Stand in a quiet space placing your right hand lightly on your heart.

Now, imagine the sun's rays are streaming through your head filling your upper body with warmth, energy and light.

At the same time, your feet are growing long roots that spiral into the earth sucking in warm, moist energy from the ground through your lower body. The light and the earth energy meet in your torso, filling your gut and heart with the most powerful, loving energy that flows around the body. Target all this energy to flow through your arms into your hands. Feel what it is like to receive your own loving energy.

How is it when the hands are slowly taken away?

Do this for three minutes daily.

Be Aware and Attentive to Your Body

'Awareness' is being attentive to your feelings and noticing which part of the body they are located within. Remember when you were in pain in the past?

Tony was never consciously aware of his left little finger until he broke it. The feeling of pain made him very aware of it until the fracture healed! This exercise makes you aware of feelings within your body. Carol used it recently when she was told a good friend had died unexpectedly. Within seconds of hearing the news, she felt a pain in her right kidney; what she thought was the trapped emotions of her sadness about her friend. Then, she recalled as a child when her grandmother was dying of cancer, she had gone into hospital with gallstones and they found she also had lung cancer. It was the last time Fiona saw her alive. She was dying to go to the toilet and held it in until her kidneys ached because she understood it would be the last time she'd ever see her again. The body-mind memory of her grandmother's death was triggered by her friend's death.

In this exercise, we are first going to focus on your 'Awareness' about a recent negative feeling you have had about somebody or something. Then we are going to be 'Attentive' to it and neutralise it.

If you have a negative feeling e.g. shock, grief or pain, note where this feeling is in your body. If it helps, give that feeling a colour and a shape to identify it more easily. Place your right hand a few centimetres lower and move the feeling inside you to the new spot where your hand is. Repeat the action until bit by bit, the feeling has moved down your body through one of your legs and into your foot. Move it into your toes and with your hands, pull on your toes until the feeling is outside you on the ground. Now stamp on the ground to squash that feeling.

Practice 'Awareness'

Remember whatever has happened in the past, is in the past. All is calm in the now and if you feel yourself slipping back into the emotions of a previous moment or worries for the future, breathe deeply and slowly and say to yourself: 'This will pass.' Doing this for three minutes in the quiet whilst relaxing and feeling your energy in your feet, will improve things. Also, the mindful walking exercise you did in 'Steps to Improve Your Quality of THINKing' page 29, will help.

Understand Past Feelings

Best-selling author and writer about depression, Alexanda Massey[10] introduced me to this technique.

Choose a difficult relationship and a related event from the past. Describe about how you felt at the time using one word only e.g. angry, sad, hopeless, ignored. Put these words down on paper in the hand you don't usually write with. Keep going until there are no more words to write. These are the words of your 'hurt child'. Now, in your preferred writing hand, create a letter to that child explaining from this perspective what was happening. Read both pieces back slowly to yourself and then go on a walk to process what you have learned.

Manage Negative Feelings

When feelings occur, initially, they are in a 'raw state' and can be all-consuming. In the case of anger, Thich Nhat Hanh[11] talks about letting it 'cook'. It needs attention from you. You do this in a similar way to the Creative Process described on page 48. Observe the anger by letting it incubate. It will change from its raw state and start to 'cook'. Then you begin to understand why you are angry (illuminate) and if you wait patiently, it will transmute into positive energy of understanding and compassion. Then, you can put it to good use in a positive way (verify) to understand the situation. Then, make a 'mindful' choice on your course of action (see FEEL the Future section on the next page).

If the emotion is too strong to control at present, be kind to yourself. Practice mindful walking or relaxing and say to yourself: 'I am angry and I'm suffering. I'm doing my best right now and things will get better.'

Forgive Yourself and Others

Write a letter to someone you have hurt or allowed yourself to be hurt by. Focus on the impact on your feelings and actions. Construct the letter so you understand in yourself the emotional impact in you:

- Explain your hurt e.g. I felt hurt/sad/disappointed when I/you did....
- Show your remorse e.g. I'm sorry that I did....I didn't realise that....
- Apologise e.g. Please forgive me for....
- Clarify what you really want e.g. what I really want is ....

Consider whether there is anything you can do right now to remedy the situation. It could be that the person or people involved are no longer in your life, so you can't do anything.

If they are, sending a version of this letter or making contact by another means could be an option. Or perhaps, taking no action, being satisfied you have forgiven yourself and that person, is enough.

You can now burn the letter, leave it in a pot of water until it disintegrates or mix it with soil and bury it in the garden (or a pot if you don't have a garden) and plant a herb or flower in it.

FEEL the Future

FEELing Positive

The next step is to develop positive feelings for a healthy body 'memory'.

Use Your Emotional Intelligence

Daniel Goleman[12] talks about the five emotional and social competencies:

1 Self-awareness.
2 Self-regulation.
3 Motivation.
4 Empathy.
5 Social skills.

Sometimes, we can be aware of the self and ignore the feelings of others, and/or manage others at the expense of managing ourselves.

These five cornerstones are inter-connected when you display high emotional intelligence. Awareness of self and other, managing self and relationship with the other are all balanced.

'Our Hearts Touch.'

This is similar to 'My Heart Touch' but this time you are going to do this exercise with someone you love.

Stand with a partner and face each other, placing your right hand lightly on their heart. (Always check with the person if they are comfortable to let you do this. If they feel uncomfortable, place your hand about three inches away from their body but still over their heart.) Then put your left hand on their back so that it is in the same place as the right hand. Your hands are the equivalent of the two slices of bread and their body is the filling for the sandwich!

Now, imagine the sun's rays are streaming through your head filling your upper body with warmth, energy and light.

At the same time, your feet are growing long roots that spiral into the earth sucking in warm, moist energy from the ground through your lower body. The light and the earth energy meet in your torso, filling your gut and heart with the most powerful, loving energy that flows around the body. Target all this energy to flow through your arms into your hands. Let the energy pass through you into your partner. Both of you just be with each other in that moment.

Feel what it is like to give your loving energy to someone and feel what it is like to receive the 'other's' energy.

How is it when the hands are slowly taken away?

Do this for three minutes and then swap. Repeat for a further three minutes.

When you get used to the technique, you can practice giving and receiving together. By standing side onto each other, you can both touch each other's back and the heart simultaneously. You are passing your love into someone else and receiving theirs. It's about learning how to pass positive feelings between you and another.

Forming Healthy Relationships and Managing the Unhealthy Interactions

Re-consider the list of people close to you in the Ranges Section (see page 22) e.g. partner, children, parents, siblings, close and distant family, friends, work colleagues, acquaintances.

Look again at the Scales you gave them.

Work through the Scale One unhealthy relationships on your list. Consider each person in turn. Ask yourself: "Why is my relationship with x (name) unhealthy? "

Imagine, smell or feel you have a burning red fire deep in your belly and from it a wisp of black smoke comes from you, attaching you to this person.

Consider whether you would like to release yourself from this person temporarily or permanently. Then say: "I release you" and either with one blow or fan of the hand, waft the smoke away. If you decide to reconnect with them at some point in the future, imagine you have an orb full of white smoke resting just above your head. Pull a strand out like you are spinning wool and when your hand has pulled enough out so your hand is in front of your face, blow on the strand of white smoke over to this person saying: "I re-attach myself to you." Take note where the smoke strand attaches to them e.g. the head (THINK), heart (FEEL), gut (CREATE), whole body (BELIEVE). If it is the heart for example, consider how you can relate to them through FEEL, noting all of the Ranges affecting FEEL. Your relationship will become and stay positive if you do this.

Most people should try to have more average or healthy feelings Range relationships in their life. To form and maintain these relationships, complete the following exercise:

Write an 'I love me' list. Write down all the things that make you happy in your life and give thanks for this. Write down how you plan to take care of yourself and love yourself more. Then, write down how you plan to involve certain 'healthy' people in your life in doing what you love.

Start doing what you love and expect to make new 'healthy' friends in addition to those you already have!

Have Fun

Consider the last time you had fun. What were you doing? List three ways you like to have fun and three things you'd like to try as they might be fun.

Commit to doing one of them each month. Review in six months time what difference this has made to your feelings.

Eat Healthily, Drink Sensibly and Exercise Regularly

Add more fruit and vegetables, nuts and whole grains to your diet. Eat more fish and less meat. Drink more water. Consume alcohol, saturated fats and dairy products ONLY in moderation.

Music

Play or listen to happy music to lighten the mood. Dance spontaneously to music whenever you can.

Have someone who loves you be with you who is not directly involved in the situation.

Touch Others and Let Them Touch You

Be more tactile with people. If you have pets, sit with them and pat/stroke them.

Take Part in a 360 Feelings Circle

This is for a minimum of 4 people you feel close to. Each participant will share their feelings about a relationship they want to develop/change/improve and the total time for the circle of four will be two hours. Add an extra 30 minutes for each additional person over four members.

Begin with the first person. Allow them 10 minutes to explain the relationship, what's happened and is now going on and how it makes them feel. Do not interrupt them. Speaking alone and hearing one's voice helps the speaker make connections and illuminate the issue.

After this time, the group can question the speaker to clarify their understanding of the situation for the same amount of time. The group should not try to solve the issues raised.

Throughout this part, the participant listens without comment to the others sharing their feelings about similar relationships for 10 minutes. Finally, the participant has 10 minutes to share what they have learned from listening to themselves and the others in the group and how they may apply this to a similar situation or that specific relationship.

Throughout history, the essence of FEELing has been symbolised by the nature of the heart. Only you know what's in it. Only you can open or close it or reveal it to the world. Whilst science is now showing us a more complex story, sometimes the simplicity of powerful symbols reminds us powerfully of what's important. As Helen Keller understood, manage your feelings and the heart will go on.

Watch
Depak Chopra talking about the steps you can take to release emotional toxicity. www.youtube.com (search for 'Deepak Chopra Toxic Emotions').

Section Five: CREATE

"Be brave enough to live creatively. The creative is the place where no one else has ever been." (Alan Alda.)

- Your creative expression and use of imagination. The ability to generate new ideas and possibilities. To dream. To know and appreciate beauty. **CREATE**.

Carol the Creative

Carol loved art at school, until she was fifteen when Mr. Newberry replaced her teacher.

"Class, spend the lesson drawing this chair." He placed a plastic chair on top of his desk opened his newspaper and spent the next hour reading it.

For her birthday, Carol had been given a book about the Impressionist painters by her grandmother. She loved the colours the artists used, so vibrant they shimmered with energy and aliveness. In her head, Carol imagined the picture of a chair she'd seen painted by Van Gogh and tried to create the same feel in the boring plastic chair that stood squat in front of her. She pulled out a box of coloured pencils and began to draw quickly as she was inspired by her vision. Ten minutes before the lesson ended, Mr. Newberry got up to inspect their work.

" This is not the chair." He screamed at Carol. "I told you to draw a replica of it." He gave Carol a fail mark. From that moment on, Carol decided she was no good at art and she changed class and took up other studies.

As she got older and left home, Carol never forgot the Van Gogh chair. The life-force emanating from this inanimate object remained as a strong impression so wherever she lived and worked, Carol brought an artists palette of colour, texture and shape to her environment in an original, ingenious way.

One day, when she was on a train to London, Mr. Newberry walked past her in the aisle.

"Aren't you Carol Taylor?" he asked. When Carol said "yes", he replied: "I always regretted your changing subjects and dropping out of art class. You were by far and away the best student I'd seen in a long time."

It can be argued the world is moving away from the Age of the Thinker (the Industrial Revolution, the Internet and the Information Age) into the Creative Age. We face huge challenges e.g., the environment, globalisation, economic stability. Thinking inside the box or altering the existing paradigm is a temporary sticking plaster. We need to shift into a new space and we need creative, innovative and inventive people with new ideas to do this. To achieve this, people need to be trained to work with their imagination, to be open to possibilities, to see issues from different angles and perspectives. Society needs people to make things that are both useful and beautiful, that optimise our precious resources.

What Influences CREATEing?

Roger Sperry[13] found that the brain could be divided into right and left hemispheres and each had different functions. Your left brain is the logical side, working like a serial processor with its focus on words and logic. It likes to analyse information in sequence. Your right brain is like a parallel processor. It works better with dimension and colour, taking several pieces of information and piecing them together. It works with pictures and movement.

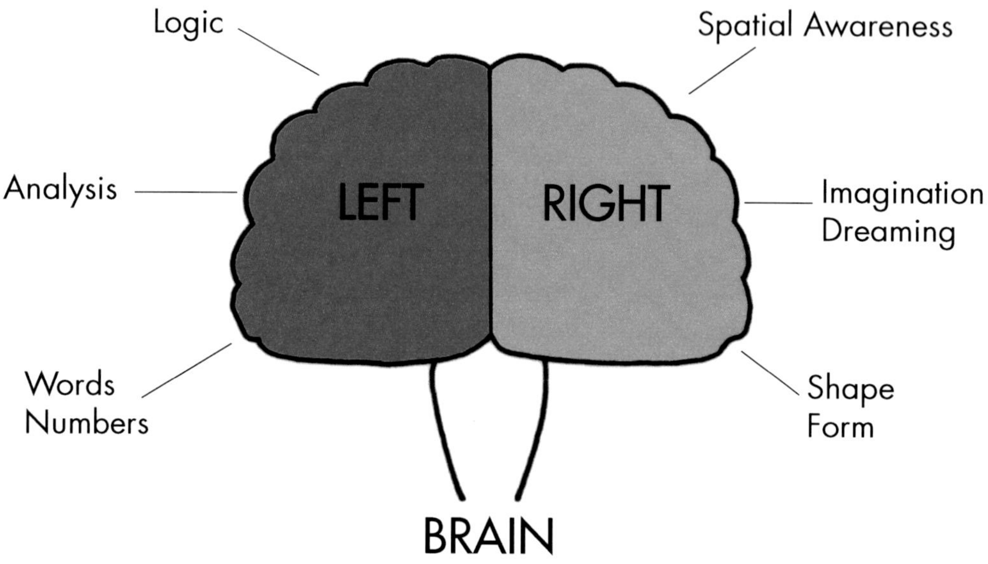

Watch
Neurologist Jill Bolte-Taylor describing what happened to her as she experiences a major stroke which shut down her logical left brain, leaving her for a while working entirely from her creative right brain hemisphere. www.youtube.com (search for Jill Bolte-Taylor 'How it Feels to have a Stroke').

The creative right brain has not been given the precedence of the logical right side. Yet, creativity has given the world some of the most amazing breakthroughs in arts, science and economics. Artistic inspiration of the kind Picasso had is only one form of creativity. This 'divine creative talent' is very rare and comes with a lot of practice and perspiration.

Here are some of the sources of creativity [14]:

By association	Combining things differently or in a new order as James Dyson[15] has used cyclone technology to reinvent domestic appliances e.g. the vacuum, fan, hand-drier.
By reversal	Doing the opposite to the norm as Dick Fosbury did when he 'flopped' backwards over a high-jump increasing the height jumped.
By inversion	Charles Handy[16] in his paper 'the Age of Unreason', says the invention of the chimney had a great impact on society because it meant heat could be channelled into rooms resulting in more privacy and independent living.
By chance/accident	Friedrich Kekule[17] dozed in his chair by the fire, trying to solve the riddle of what was the chemical structure of benzene. As he nodded, he dreamt of the twining serpents on a ring, whirling in the flames. Suddenly, in the dream, the serpents caught each other's tail and formed a circle.

By chance/accident — Einstein[18] was said to develop the Theory of Relativity when he imagined travelling on a beam of light backwards in time. In reality, many of these 'accidents' or flukes are the result of years of hard work and experiments by people at the top of their game.

Creativity takes you away from monotony and routine. It provides you with excitement, harmony and a different kind of concentration. Yet, as soon as most people hear or see the word CREATE, they close down, believing to be creative means you have to be a great actor, artist, dancer or painter. But as you now know from the above definitions, there are many more ways of showing your creativity than artistic expression.

You can bring CREATE into daily life any time you want. Think about a person choosing, then hanging a roll of wallpaper in their home. The focus and concentration they have is centered on their dexterous hands and is a creative act. Creativity can link the mind and body, bringing it together in harmony digging the soil, writing a diary, painting a wall, humming a tune in the shower or baking a cake. We all have moments of creativity, from when we get up and choose what clothes to wear!

If you have scored CREATE as your Home Quarter, do you recognise elements of Carol the Creative in your behaviour and outlook on life?

Who are the 'CREATEives' in your personal and work life? What would it be like to just have a group of CREATEives in a room?

Consider your interactions with CREATEives. What could you do to get better results from your relationship with them?

How much CREATEing are you doing to the exclusion of the other Quarters?

CREATE Ranges

Here are examples of Healthy, Average and Unhealthy CREATEives so you can map yourself against them and improve the quality of your CREATE Range.

Healthy Creatives

- They dream of a better future and are open to possibilities.
- They imagine, encourage and allow new ideas to form.
- They combine the old in different ways to create the new.
- They express their creativity through creative works e.g. artistic, cultural, social.
- They are colourful, expressive, engaging people, fun to be around.
- They take calculated risks when the opportunities are worth it.

Average Creatives

- They are good at applying creative thinking techniques to problem-solving.
- They cope well with change because often it requires creative solutions and a greater tolerance of creativity.

- Their environment reflects their creative tendencies e.g. thought into home and work exterior and interior design and the sensory landscape.
- They invent, draw, design and engineer.
- They become over-protective of their 'creation', viewing the world as 'misguided' when nobody wants to take on their handiwork.
- They get frustrated when their ideas are mocked or not listened to. This is followed by stress and anger.

Unhealthy Creatives

- They may have a great idea or product but they lack the managerial or business skills to bring them to market.
- The creative process gives them such a buzz, their health (diet, sleep) suffer.
- They may take artificial substances e.g. drugs, alcohol in an effort to sustain creative 'highs.'
- Creatives tend to suffer more depression and other mental health issues than average.

Danger Signal

That the thing they are creating is consistently more important than family, friends and the things they used to find important. They lose regular sleep, eating, exercising patterns.

How to Make a Creative Happy

- Give them a problem and some time to understand its real/true cause before solving it.
- Don't close a CREATIVE down. Give them the physical and mental space to dream and express their ideas.
- Listen to them even if it seems fanciful to you. They might just be on to something.
- Let them present in the now rather than making them go away and reflect and come back later.

Help CREATE Healthily

There are several ways to move CREATE from the Unhealthy Range:

- Gain balance by doing THINK programmes. If you are an artist or creative entrepreneur, learn business-planning, marketing and communication skills.
- Learn structured problem-solving techniques e.g. by reading books on lateral thinking and creative thinking.
- Set aside creative time within the day and then spend the rest of it doing exercise, other work and pastimes.
- Do a voluntary activity to benefit the community.

Steps to Improve Your Quality of CREATEing

Adults forget how creative they once were. It's still there, but over time, it has been masked or covered up.

Think back to when you were at school, in your early adulthood and to the age you are now. What creative things have you done?

Write them down and then think about how much they may have influenced how you view things and how they make you feel.

Do you still do creative things? If not, what creativity could you introduce into your life that you have done in the past, or maybe something new?

Think about a problem you have at work or home. Can you see if you applied a bit of creative thinking it might help you?

Solving a problem: Let's use a 360 Wisdom approach to this.

Solving Problems From Quarter Perspectives

Sometimes an unexpected problem comes along and you don't know how to solve it. By considering it from a different Quarter in the 360 Circle could help you unlock new ways of resolving it or coming to terms with the issues it raises.

Imagine you are at the centre of the 360 Circle (even better, if you can, physically stand and step into the centre of an imaginary circle).

To your left in front of you is the THINK quarter. To your right, FEEL. Over your left shoulder is CREATE and over your right, BELIEVE.

Now, identify a problem or difficulty you are experiencing in your life right now. It may be a health, relationship, work-related or money issue or something that involves one or more of these!

Step into each Quarter (THINK, FEEL, CREATE, BELIEVE) in turn and imagine you can only see the problem from a one Quarter at a time, answer the following:

- How would a THINKER (FEELER, CREATIVE, BELIEVER) interpret the nature of the problem?
- How could the problem be solved from the THINKER (FEELER, CREATIVE, BELIEVER) perspective?
- What have you learned about your problem and its possible resolution from the Quarter's perspectives?

If you have found it difficult to work out of one of the Quarters, this is because it's your weakest, your Away Quarter. Try working through your problem with someone you suspect or know has it as their Home Quarter.

CREATE Now

1. Mimicking

THINKERS, FEELERS and BELIEVERS assume there's great mystery and mystique to being creative. This is not true. Often, by copying or mimicking creative techniques, you can quickly master the creative process by watching and learning from the best. This is what nature does all the time. Cubs model their parents hunting techniques and birds learn to sing this way by mimicking others of the same species.

Artists have a style that can be copied (you can learn these techniques in books by Tony Buzan[19] and Drawing on the Right Side of the Brain[20].There are numerous books on how to generate ideas e.g. Edward De Bono[21] and you can pick up a lot by reading about great creative entrepreneurs like Oprah Winfrey[22] or Richard Branson[23].

2. Process

There is a defined creative process. It involves doing many of the opposite things you are used to doing when you THINK. First, (as you have already learned,) empty the mind by relaxing and acknowledging any stray thoughts and just letting them pass by. Then, enjoy the empty 'mind space' and allow new ideas to come. Suspend any critical thoughts and let yourself ride along staying curious and fascinated by the ideas that come. Let the idea grow and evolve until it becomes clear, then look for connections and possibilities for developing it into something useful for your life and other's. This is the creative process and is explained as follows[24]:

Preparation	Having enough of the necessary skills and knowledge plus the ability to free up the mind.
Incubation	Letting the unconscious mind take over to generate ideas.
Illumination	Allowing time to let insight in, absorbing it and reflecting until the way becomes clear.
Verification	Developing the insight or idea into a tangible product or service and putting it to use.

3. Visualise

Visualisations are a great way to open up your creativity. Try this one to see if it unlocks yours!

Imagine you are in a dark cave without any light. Be aware of the environment. It's not cold, in fact you feel nice and warm. You are not afraid, in fact you feel snug as if you have woken up from a hibernation period. Feel around the space. Can you feel the rock wall? Is it rough or smooth? Does it run with water? Now, bend down and feel the dry, sandy floor. Let it trickle through your fingers and as you do so, know that all the beliefs, feelings and memories you have about yourself are past. There is just the real you, here alone in the cave in the 'now' just being. You expect nothing and want nothing.

Look in front of you and if you are careful, you will see a tiny chink of light. This is the mouth of the cave. Walk towards it and as you do, notice the light gets brighter and the hole bigger. As you walk towards the light, know it is a special light. It is the light of creativity and this light comes from the beginning of time.

Very soon, you will be standing in the light and at the height of your creative powers.

Stand in the mouth of the cave and look out. You will see an amazing sandy beach stretching as far as your eyes can see. Its perfect, virgin sand, yet to be marked with footprints. Note how the tide causes the waves to beat rhythmically on the shore. Now match your breathing to this.

Stay in the cave even though you have the desire to rush towards the waves and be subsumed in the sea. Look down to the floor at the mouth of the cave. You will see a box. Decide what the box is like. Is it encrusted with jewels or made from plain boxwood? Is it ornately carved or made from tin?

Pick up your box. It feels heavy doesn't it?

Your box contains all the ideas you will ever need in your lifetime to solve problems, make your surroundings more pleasing, help others.

It is **your** 'creative ideas' box.

Step out of the cave onto the beach and open your box. Let the creative ideas fly out into the sunshine and note every one as they float gradually upwards.

Don't try to catch your creativity and pin it down. Just remember the creative ideas as they drift across your peripheral vision. Each one will come back to you as and when you need it.

Write down everything you experienced. What ideas did you recall?

CREATE the Future

Observe Nature

Walk outdoors and take in the view. Watch what nature does. Switch your thinking off and study what's before you. Write your observations down in a Creative Thoughts notebook. Someone before you observed the stickiness of spiders webs and the blood coagulating properties of leeches and applied them to medical science.

Work with Nature

Go foraging outdoors in silence for an hour. Pick up fallen branches, leaves, flowers, bark, stones and anything else of interest without harming the environment. Create something with the pieces by sticking or tying or twisting them into shapes for display or useful objects. Look at the natural textures, lines and curves of the materials and their use will become apparent e.g. a vessel, sculpture, tool.

Make Your Routines Fun
Go food shopping and have an 'orange cream dinner' where everything consists of those colours, or choose a theme for the meal e.g. a country (Morocco) or a film (the Godfather) and cook according to your interpretation of that!

Mow your lawn side to side rather than up and down. Vacuum to the songs of your favourite pop singer. Be spontaneous. Embrace the unpredictable and quirky!

Use Your Hands
Feel the earth. How long is it since soil ran through your fingers. Plant something and watch it grow. If you don't have a garden, use a window-box or some pots in your window. Try dancing, a craft (anything from bricklaying to mosaics, salsa to stained glass.) There's something immensely satisfying in bringing something to life and watching it grow.

Section Six: BELIEVE

"Simply notice the order of things. Work within it rather than against it. For to try and change what is only sets up resistance". (Lao Tzu)

- The journey of self-improvement. To find the joy in life and your purpose.

Bridget the Believer

Bridget sat in her favourite seat in the garden letting sunlight flicker across her face until her laughter-lined skin was warmed.

For a while, she took in her surroundings until she became part of them. She was not an observer looking in on this stunning natural world.

She had longed since learned how to enter this dimension with ease.

'Today is the day I leave this world'. She thought.

Her arm raised the crystal glass with nothing sinister in it apart from honey-coloured wine, perfectly chilled. How old her hands looked she noted. The skin was pitted with liver spots, flesh shrunken to show sinew and shape of bone.

She was an old lady, almost ninety five. She chose this beautiful day to die.

In her hedonistic, lost youth at the plantation, she would never have imagined she'd live beyond thirty. But instead she had lived a fulfilled life for many years.

She toasted the sky and drank deeply, her palate bursting with the dryness of the wine combined with a hint of apricot and alcohol.

She remembered the day when everything changed due to a combination of circumstances that stopped her being scared to try out anything new or different. With hindsight, her fear of failure had been unfounded.

She'd made a conscious decision to find and live her truth. That was the key, to live a higher purpose beyond ego and all it's trappings of finery and flattery. She'd believed all would be well. As a result, she found herself a wealthy, loved woman.

She put her glass down on the table and patted the book lying next to it. It contained her blue-print or treasure map for others to follow for a joyful life.

Her granddaughter would call later, would know what to do with her body and the body of evidence she was leaving behind for others to share, to transform their consciousness and their lives.

Her face was reddening with the sun and wine. Bridget reached over and covered her head with a white, wide-brimmed hat. She giggled at the absurdity of her wanting to cover up when in a few minutes, it wouldn't matter at all.

She was ready. She allowed the tiredness she'd felt for a while to envelop her. Her eyes closed, a brief smile playing across her lips as she slowly shut down her body.

A light breeze rippled through the trees making them rustle as if in a secret conversation. Perfume wafted from tea roses, jasmine and lavender in nearby flowerbeds and fluttered across the pages of the book called 'The Whole Truth' that lay open by her side.

What Influences BELIEVEing?

THINK and FEEL quarters have been about understanding you and your relationship to the external world. In CREATE, you explored the notion of how to release your creative energy into the world. BELIEVE is about doing and acting *for* the world, not just for yourself. BELIEVE is about much bigger picture stuff than your ego. It's about knowing who you are and what your life's purpose is. Then you can learn how to connect up with other people and communities who BELIEVE to work across boundaries beyond your known map of the world to make a difference to the collective good of the planet.

360 Wisdom believes everyone is born with a purpose. Some may never look for theirs, others may know it at birth or find it on their life's journey.

Far less people have BELIEVE as their Home Quarter for many reasons. Daily life is a constant struggle and most people don't have the space or time to work out who they are and what they can offer to others. Often, they only realise this and gain a sense of inner peace with age. There are some exceptions. Some/all people are born with a clear sense of purpose and direction. Bridget knew from an early age she was connected in a far deeper way to nature than many people around her. She had an innate sense of purpose and knew her time would come to put it into practice even though for many years, she lived by another's rules (her father's).

She knew what she wanted to accomplish. She knew her gift. By accepting the truth in herself and being true to it and all others, Bridget is able to be herself and live life to the full. Removing the second E in BELIEVE gives, 'BE LIVE'. Live in the moment, for the moment, alive in the moment!

BELIEVE is about expressing who you are every day of your life to your fullest potential. You don't have to wait until old age to BELIEVE.

BELIEVE is not about religious practice or faith (although religious people can also BELIEVE, so can atheists and agnostics!). It is about you being you and doing your 'thing' out there as a fully present and sentient human being!

If you lose BELIEVE, it feels terrible. You feel disconnected; the living dead. If you gain BELIEF, it's like you are awake and alive for the first time.

If you have scored BELIEVE as your Home Quarter, you will primarily run your inner and outer worlds from an holistic perspective where you see the big picture, the good in all people and the benefits of 'making a difference'. How much do you recognise elements of Bridget the BELIEVEr in your behaviour and outlook on life?

Who are the 'BELIEVErs' in your personal and work life? What would it be like to just have a group of BELIEVErs in a room?

Consider your interactions with BELIEVErs. What could you do to get better results from your relationship with them?

How much BELIEVEing are you doing to the exclusion of the other Quarters?

BELIEF Ranges

Here are some examples of healthy BELIEVE you can map yourself against as well as improving your quality of BELIEVE by trying the exercises below.

Healthy Believing

- Serve not self is the motto.
- Believers see the 'not yet seen' so their passion spots a gap in something.
- They live authentic, congruent lives i.e. they say what they mean, mean what they say and do what they say!
- They use peripheral vision to bring in more and varied bits of information helping to make links and connections.

Average Believing

- They have a vocation and love it.
- They are holistic thinkers, looking for the bigger picture and trying to understand the totality of it.
- They make quick decisions based on competence and faith in their abilities.
- Key to them is making a contribution.
- They hate being controlled by others.
- They play on a big stage, opening themselves up to big risks and rewards.

Unhealthy Believing

- They waste time waiting for the 'truth' to reveal itself.
- Sometimes, they can get cult-like about the truth.
- When they 'big themselves up' they can often take themselves too seriously, developing a 'God complex.'
- They can go mad trying to comprehend the universe.

Danger Signal

The default state of a Believer is someone who is tolerant of others. They stand out in a crowd and are prepared to lose everything for a cause. Danah Zohar and Ian Marshall[25] in their book 'Spiritual Capital: Wealth we can live by' call this 'Field Independence.' It is also about standing out against the dictates of your mind and feelings. Once someone loses this perspective and becomes aware of power relations between people, they have lost their BELIEF.

Help BELIEVE Healthily

There are several ways to move from the unhealthy BELIEVING Range.

1. Quiet

Take 20 minutes at the beginning and end of each day to be quiet. Sit still with your eyes closed and try to calm, then empty your mind. Any stray thoughts, note them and let them pass by. The more you do this, the quicker and easier it becomes. You will feel refreshed and more alert and aware.

2. Set the Day

Set and complete the day. Spend a few minutes after the above exercise deciding how you want to be on this day and review what happened and what you've learned at its end.

3. Kindness

Make conscious interventions. Try and be kind to someone every day.

4. Routines

Be aware of your routines and try to break them up or alter them.

How BELIEVE Originated

Through the ages, human beings have worshipped a higher being, sensing there is a greater power on the outside of us. BELIEVE people sense a similar power within themselves and others. Great BELIEVErs seem to radiate a power and spirit so strong, they seem really *alive*. People are drawn to their energy.

Yet, at the same time, they seem to be 'other-worldly' as if they exist in another dimension; straggling two worlds of waking and of sleep. "Those who have compared our life to a dream were right.... We sleeping wake, and waking sleep." [26]

What You Believed

Once, you BELIEVEd in yourself, before the external world told you your dreams were futile and you convinced yourself this was true. Let's re-connect with your belief in yourself.

BELIEVE Now

This exercise will help you now to re-define your talent in a more mature way.

Get yourself into the 360 relaxed state (see page 11) where you can feel the energy of your creative, feeling, thinking, and believing centres.

Imagine you are walking up a steep hill. Over the brow of the hill you see laid out before you a golden city, its turrets glinting in the sun. It is Camelot. You walk down towards it and enter the North Gate. The inner walls are decorated with fine tapestries and flags billow gently in the breeze. This is a happy place.

You are directed to pass through a courtyard leading to King Arthur's Palace. In the centre of the City rests a Grand Hall. Within the Hall is the Round Table.

King Arthur sits at his place, his stone seat carved with a lion's mane headrest and clawed arm rests. He is deep in thought. The King smiles and beckons you over. "Tell me who I am and why I'm here" you say. Arthur replies. You note his words in your being and move on as directed.

At the southern end of the city, you find Sir Lancelot. He sits alone on a wall feeling deeply the anguish of lost love. He smiles and beckons you over. "Tell me who I am and why I'm here" you say. Lancelot replies. You note his words in your being and move on as directed.

You head east and find Sir Gawain. He has recently slain the Green Knight and ponders the link between birth, death and creativity. "Tell me who I am and why I'm here" you say. Gawain replies. You note his words in your being and move on as directed.

Finally, as the sun sets, you find yourself heading west out of Camelot towards the coast. For it is said a mystical man, a believer in the old magic, lives a hermit life in a cave on the beach. You enter the cave. It is warm, humid and perfumed with drying herbs. An old man with a stooped back looks at you. His eyes are afire with spirit and belief that goodness and love will overcome all. "Tell me who I am and why I'm here" you say. Merlin replies. You note his words in your being and move on as directed.

You find yourself sitting by a large lake as dusk comes. You feel calmed by the still, velvet waters. An arm arises from the lake and in it is a sword. The arm becomes a torso and so on until a whole body emerges. It is a beautiful woman with kind eyes. The Lady of the Lake beckons you over. "Tell me who you are and why you are here", she asks. Tell her.

Write down all your thoughts, impressions and experiences on this journey. Leave them to 'cook' for a week and then consider them again. What insights did you learn from this journey? Do you get a sense of the area you want to focus on? If you did, can you refine it/hone it down into a field/work/profession you want to spend time in? Is this something that is work, a hobby, voluntary service? What do you need to learn or do to find out more about getting involved?

Make an action plan of all the steps you need to consider to learn more and place a time-frame of no more than a year around this.

Create a Vision Board. Transfer all your hopes, dreams (waking and sleeping) and aspirations onto a large sheet of paper in words, drawings and images. Cut out pictures from magazines and newspapers that reflect and represent your desires. If a phrase, quote or line from a song inspires you, use it. When you spot something new that resonates, add it to your Board.

Your Vision Board will provide you with a focus and intention that we will use later on in Section 8: the Diamond.

Stop Negative Beliefs

For all the mental and emotional 'baggage' you have accumulated over your life, here are two ways to dispel them so that you maintain your essence and keep on track. As you get closer to understanding and acting upon your potential, you will find obstacles mount. This is because your thoughts and emotions are changing onto fresh, new more authentic pathways. As the old ways are firmly entrenched, they will try to assert their authority over the new. You can overcome them.

Write Them Out

Carol realised she could start up a garden-design business focusing on creating spaces that produced herbs and easy to grow fruit and vegetables. Initially, she was excited and energised by the prospect and then doubts set in. One of her major issues was she knew she'd have to advertise and sell herself to her family, friends and complete strangers. This was an area she'd never ventured into and she believed she lacked sales skills. Selling became a big issue and the more she worried about it, the more anxious she became. She was just about to give up on the whole idea until she decided to write about her fears.

Spend some time identifying the issues preventing you from believing in yourself. Follow the example of selling but apply your topic accordingly. Write about the topic in a 'stream of consciousness' i.e. don't think about what you are putting down on paper, just let it flow.

Here are some sub-headings you can use to shift you. Substitute the word 'selling' for something you find difficult.

- Selling to me is......
- Selling to me is not.....
- I have the fear of selling because.....
- I don't have the sales I want because....
- Now read back what you have written.
- What are the key issues? How could you solve them?

Carol understood there had been a number of close relatives who'd set themselves up in various businesses that had failed spectacularly because they'd spent far too much money on the trappings of success (company cars, expensive IT equipment, staff they initially didn't need) without marketing their business and bringing in income.

She also remembered as a child her mother being plagued by door-to-door salesmen who persuaded her to buy things the family couldn't afford. As a result, she thought sales people were pushy or inadequate intellectually.

But Carol also learned from this exercise that she was a buyer of goods and services and that the people she purchased from had something she wanted or needed to buy. She purchased from companies that had integrity e.g. environmentally-conscious and from sales-staff who had integrity (they worked for businesses who had strong values).

Carol realised if she was clear about her values and wove them into her business, she could sell her ideas with conviction. She realised her fear of selling was just that 'a fear' and until she had a go, how would she know if she was any good or not? She vowed she would try her best.

Bitter Critter

Every time you make a significant leap forward in how you THINK, FEEL, CREATE, BELIEVE, you are moving away from your old self and its internal and external controls. For people who are brave enough to begin their journey of self-discovery this can cause upset with friends, family and colleagues. Seeing reality from a different perspective and trying to explain this to someone who doesn't is like describing the vast array of herbs and spices to someone only used to flavouring their food with salt and pepper!

The struggle is hard and often painful. At this stage, you start to procrastinate. Perhaps it's better to stay where you are with everyone else. It's lonely trying to become 360.

This is where Bitter Critter steps in. Just as you recognise a pattern that's so imprinted in you it's blinkered you, Bitter Critter leaps out. Bitter Critter whispers in your ear not to get rid of old, ingrained thoughts for they must be right as they've been there so long.

When Tony THINKS and is mindful he's heard his father's voice not his own, his Bitter Critter digs its nails in his neck and pinches him, reminding him to obey his elders and betters.

When Carol wants a different life experience, Bitter Critter whispers 'You don't have the right, just the responsibility to stay where you are. There are people depending on you.

Bridget's Bitter Critter is shrivelled like a mummified head. It has lips that if kissed, would be like biting into poisoned fruit. Its smile is pitted with empty spaces where the teeth have decayed away. Hairy warts sprout all over Bitter Critter's body and it smells like it's never been in contact with any water apart from its own sweat.

Bitter Critter is the 'head' voice of generations of ancestors and all the people influential in your life. Whenever you're about to make a major breakthrough, a change of direction or a different choice, your Bitter Critter will tell you to stay put or worse still, do the opposite. Bitter Critter is the *false self*, the 'thing' we've become attached to. It is not who you really *are*.

When you listen to Bitter Critter there's a wisdom in the words. It sounds like the collective voice of all the Bitter Critter relatives, friends, role-models you were told to abide by.

Learn to listen but not hear – to take into account but not necessarily to act upon Bitter Critter. Learn to look for the perception called your 'reading consciousness' which is a knowing, kind presence that enjoys sitting quietly in the sun, walking though the fields, concentrating on creative things and has balanced feelings. Eckhart Tolle describes that what lies beyond that is: " *...a vast realm of intelligence beyond thought, that thought is only a tiny aspect of that intelligence. You also realise that all the things that truly matter – beauty, love, creativity, joy, inner-peace – arise from the mind. You begin to awaken.*" [27]

Only then does Bitter Critter disappear in a puff of smoke. If Bitter Critter materialises again, stand in front of the toilet, pick it off your shoulder, throw Bitter Critter down the pan, flush the chain and close the lid.

The more Bitter Critter drowns, the more its voice gets weaker and weaker until one day it stops.

When I'm 360, my Bitter Critter is not there at all. This is because I exist in balance, aware of my human and being nature in a far richer emotional, mental and creative space connected to the vast intelligence Eckhart so beautifully describes.

Draw your Bitter Critter. Give your Bitter Critter a name. Write all over its body all the things you find irritating about your Bitter Critter. When you have finished, either rip up your picture or burn it and watch your fears disappear into the bin or up in smoke into the air.

Believe in Yourself

We tend to believe the worst things about ourselves and assume people we know perceive us in the same way. Here's an exercise that gets you to externalise your essence and explores what you assume others perceive you are. When you have completed it, go back and check with them if your understanding about you and their understanding of you matches!

Find the sheet of paper you wrote all the words your friends, family, colleagues and you use to describe yourself and recall the words you highlighted.

Notice the common words and phrases (those that jump off the page at you). Make a list of these. Repeat the words out loud until you have a sense which ones are the strongest representation for you.

Look back to your Vision Board and any notes you made from the ideas box visualisation in CREATE and any notes or thoughts you had from the Camelot visualisation and add these to your list. Can you see new patterns emerging for the 'new you'?

Now turn these into a 360 **Essence Statement**.

For example: If the word or phrase 'helpful' comes up and you feel this strongly inside, this is one of your essence notes.

Try to externalise this e.g. I want to help people.

Now consider 'how' you can help people until something resonates (you get a 'gut instinct' this is good for you.)

In this example 'I want to feed the hungry' may be a better result.

Now think of a metaphor that captures the essence e.g. Growing food crops and harvesting them feeds people. 'I am the crop that keeps the hungry fed and nourished.'
Then turn this essence metaphor into an action e.g. I nourish the hungry.

Consider 'how' you can do this. Could you give some volunteer time to a local charity? Should you be working in a job where you can do this? Does this involve travel? Let your imagination soar and see what you come up with. Don't think of barriers and obstacles.

Write your 'Essence Statement' on a postcard. On a second postcard, write 'three things I will do to achieve my essence'. Ask a trusted friend to keep them for a month and post the cards back to you.

When you receive them, make a note of how you feel.

After you have received your postcards, wait a further week and then write a 250 word summary that could be used for the rear jacket cover of your autobiography. Explain who you are, what you have achieved and the way you have gone about doing it.

How to Make a BELIEVER Happy

- Ask them to make connections across social, political and cultural boundaries.
- Give them a community issue to solve.
- Put them in front of people as ambassadors for a cause.

Your Values: Navigation Tools for BELIEVE

People with a BELIEVE Home Quarter have a strong sense of personal values and incorporate them into everything they do. It is part of their essence and can't be avoided. Believers have a vision about what they want to achieve and why. This may be determined in part by a deep knowledge of their personal values that are used as their moral compass, plus the knowledge of how to translate this vision into tangible things in the world.

All the Quarters have values. These are personal values: all the things that you deem to be worthy and important for you. Whenever you move out of your Home Quarter, your values act as your guide. They are your moral 'sonar'. Whenever you meet people who share similar values, you feel comfortable with them. If you try to live without them, it's doesn't take too long before you feel so uncomfortable, you know you are not being true to yourself. All of the Quarters have a set of predominant values (see below), but only a BELIEVEr lives them to the letter as if their life depended on it.

Here's some examples of values: fairness, family, creativity, connectivity, reputation, humour, integrity, status, wealth, reciprocity, honour, fun.

Most people don't know what their values are until something happens to them or someone they empathise with. For example, Carol couldn't get her child into their local school, making her angry. She realised she was cross because she felt their treatment was unjust. This value of 'justice' Carol realised, was important to her as she expected to treat others and be treated by them in a fair, impartial way.

If you had to write down your six most important values, what would they be?

Ask yourself how many of these six have been influenced by your parents, friends and workplace. How many of them are really your own?

Write down the values someone with their Home Quarter would have in THINK, FEEL, CREATE and BELIEVE.

Predominant Values

THINK Values

Expect a Thinker to value wealth, entrepreneurialism, reputation, status, qualifications, achievement, toughness, integrity, taking risks, choice, networks, being persuasive.

FEEL Values

Expect a Feeler to value family, connectivity (to people), compassion, companionship, passion, justice, fun, helping others, safety, comfort.

CREATE Values

Expect a Creative to value ideas, personal and collective expression, imagination, dreams, expression, curiosity, innovation, making connections (between the abstract), space, independence, non-conformity.

BELIEVE Values

Expect a Believer to value solitude, peace, freedom, space, well-being, free-will, harmony, tranquility, connectivity (to nature).

Be aware as you learn how to move around your Away Quarters and incorporate them into your life, you will begin to adopt some of their Predominant Values as well. Some of them will stick with you. Others will be there for a short time as you experience the Quarter and move on.

A useful way of knowing how far you have come with 360 Wisdom is to check your values on a regular basis (e.g. every six months) to see the changes in your values set. When Carol had spent time with Tony learning about how to THINK more about turning her creative ideas into a business, she decided to sell her skills in garden design. Tony helped her develop a business plan and set up her company. A year later, when Carol left her teaching job to work in her business full-time, she repeated the personal values exercise you are about to do and found that her reputation and ability to create wealth were now important.

These new values were added to her Home Quarter values of creativity and authenticity. When Carol took on a job it would have to let her be creative, express herself and provide her with a living wage. If work came in that didn't this, Carol could choose to do it knowing that she was compromising her values, the essence of what she deemed important.

Finding Your True Values

There are two ways you can find your personal values. Try them both and compare results. See which one works best for you.

Put yourself into the relaxed state. Then say to yourself: 'My being will tell me my true values.' Now begin.

Write down a list of values as quickly as you can. When you hit a 'writer's block', draw a horizontal line across the page and wait. Be patient and trust you will find more. Start writing again. When you hit a second block, draw a second horizontal line across the page. Trust yourself once more. Keep writing. When you have finished, lay your paper to one side.

Put yourself into the relaxed state. Recall once more the time when you were most happy.

Recall as much as you can about your impression.

Who were you with? What were you doing? Why was it so good for you?

Write down as much as you can recall about the experience and the essence of you as you were. How were you thinking, feeling, creating, believing? Scan your work for words that jump out at you. If they are not already values, what values do they suggest?

Write down these values.

Both these exercises should suggest lists of values.

Write down the values you have in both lists plus any that jump out at you. Try and understand what each value means to you. Give it definition by fleshing out its meaning.

Go through each value and rank it in order of how important from a scale of 1-10, (10 being the highest) it has featured in your life up until now.

Now decide what are your top ten values.

Work through how you define each value and write down their meaning.

Now decide what are your top 5 values.

From these, select your top 3 values. These have to be so strong you would fight to the death to keep them.

These are your True Values. They are who you are. They have defined how you act up until now.

Can you recognise a pattern that links your core values to the four Quarters?

Do these True Values fit your Home Quarter?

Watch
Martin Luther King was a key leader in the American Civil Rights movement. He believed in non-violent protest. He was assassinated in 1968. This is one of his greatest speeches, a man who BELIEVEd passionately in his life purpose and his cause, www.youtube.com (search for Martin Luther King 'I Have a Dream Speech').

Section Seven: Crystallisation

Full Circle

If you have reached this part of the Guide, you have travelled the 360 Wisdom Circle possibly once, twice or three times to understand the Home and Away Quarters and the Ranges. You have completed the exercises, watched the videos and I hope have read more deeply the work of some of the amazing human beings I have mentioned throughout this Guide. (More details are outlined in the *References* section on page 74 and *'People and Books That Have Inspired Me'* on page 83.) You will have also gained some insights into your inner self and how you plan to live your life from this point on.

Travelling around the 360 Wisdom Circle is a process I call *'Crystallisation'*.

When molecules in a solvent start to gather into a cluster, they reach a critical size and develop stable nuclei and a crystal forms. The type of the crystal depends on the arrangement of the atoms. There are many different types of crystal and they can be found in the natural world and produced artificially.

The parallels between this process and 360 Wisdom are that as you learn about the Four Quarters and the Ranges, the molecules in you start to become more stable. As your knowledge and understanding about yourself and your world grows, you grow in understanding. You reach a critical cluster size! Your map of the world and your ability to change your feelings and mind-set as well as take on board new ideas to develop your talent and purpose, arranges you into your unique form.

The world and your experience of it to date has been fragile and strong just like the properties of a crystal. You have seen and understood your past from all facets of your crystal. Now, you are in the present moment and things are becoming crystal clear.

Time in the 360 Circle

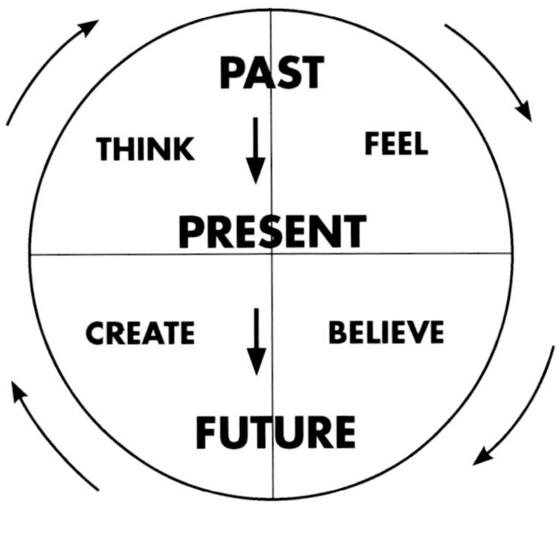

When you worked your way around the introduction to the 360 Wisdom Quarters; THINK, FEEL, CREATE, BELIEVE, you were travelling around the outer rim of the 360 Wisdom Circle. Learning something new and applying it takes a relatively long time in temporal terms (the linear way we measure time in hours, minutes and seconds, perhaps on a car journey for example).

You are also affected by 'inner-outer spin'. This is where your inner world turns slower than the outer world which gets ever faster. The vast majority of people regardless of their culture, religion, or race, generally want to stay healthy, make a living, find love and leave a legacy. The inner world of these wants and desires is 'slow' as our ancestors and descendents will want much the same. What has changed is the pace of the outer world. Over the course of history, the outer world has become ever faster. Industrialisation, mass communication and travel, innovation and the scarcity of resources is speeding things up. That makes most people feel out of control, like a spinning top about to topple over as they try to 'square the circle' between the internal and external. It can make you feel pretty giddy, a bit like being on a merry-go-round where you feel you are travelling slowly but then you see the faces of the people watching you moving very quickly.

When you completed the in-depth exercises for each Quarter, you began a journey across the 360 Wisdom Circle. Inner-outer spin has stopped because you are steadier and have a healthier attitude to the outside world. By working through the Circle rather than going around it, you will cut the time travelled in half (the diameter of a circle is half its circumference.) This is because you are aware of who you are, what you want and how you can realise it. We waste a lot of time trying to work out these things!

During this speeded up travel (let's say the speed of sound), you move into a different understanding of past, present and future where you start to move straight for the solutions rather than focussing on all the problems and the obstacles for moving you forward.

This brings about an element of understanding and control that many people don't possess. For them, life is about being buffeted by the outside world, worrying about the past and what might be happening in the future. Life is viewed as luck or chance, not designed. Ironically, these people have total free will because they don't know who they are or where they are heading. They can *choose* to do anything they wish but they don't understand how to this from the perspective of *conscious* choice.

People who choose 360 Wisdom gain total consciousness and are able to act in the present with full knowledge and understanding of their impact on the world. At this level there is no free will. Choices become narrower until there is no choice.

But if you stayed in the present for the rest of your life, it would become hedonistic. Living 'in the now' without a thought of the future or a care for the past is a great place to be. But all you are doing is 'receiving', taking advantage of serendipity and whatever comes your way. You would have a pleasurable time, but would not be adding any value to the world and ultimately, to yourself.

Having 360 Wisdom is different. You are still present, living in the moment, but are also able to take what comes and get creative with it. This involves adding value to what comes and seeing opportunities where you can make a difference. This gives you choice about what to do next about your future. You move into the future by entering CREATE and BELIEVE to understand who you are and what you can create *for* the world. This is a place of hope and opportunity, not hedonism and self-indulgence.

When all four Quarters are understood, you will be balanced, aware and present. Then you understand that things have shifted. You know who you are and what you have to do. There is no free will here (apart from how you go about doing it) because now you are ready to assume what is fated and destined for you. How exciting and self-satisfying is that?!

Final Preparations

When people go on a journey, they usually know their destination. They have a place they aim to reach at journey's end.

We are going to keep one foot in the material world in your current 'map' using the other to take a step right off your map into a new space.

Because you have one foot in known territory and have progressed around and through the 360 Wisdom Circle at the speed of sound, standing on the Diamond prepares you to safely take a step out into the unknown.

In this instance, imagine you are like the explorers of 200 years ago, going into the Amazon or parts of Africa for the first time. These 'navigators' may not have known the territory but they had an objective in mind e.g. to find the source of the Nile and they made sure they were well prepared. They carried food and water, light, navigation equipment and things to defend themselves from illness and predators. They also carried materials to chart what they were seeing and experiencing.

They had no maps and had to navigate the unknown, recording where they had gone as they moved forward. Until they gave places, rivers, lakes and valleys a name, no names existed for them.

So, just like these pioneers, you will prepare and shape yourself and name your destination into your uncharted space in four ways:

1. Prepare Your Destination

You have your Healthy Ranges. They are there to nourish and sustain you. Feel them now.

You have your True Values. They are your navigation tools. Recall them now.

You have your light of kindness for you do everything 'for' the world, not yourself. Shine it selflessly now.

2. Shape Your Destination

This shifts you from the material to the symbolic and from this intermediate 'language' you will be able to recognise the new 'poetry' of the Diamond which is explained on page 69.

3. Creating Your Avatar

The original definition of 'Avatar' came from Hinduism. It was the manifestation of a divine being in either human or animal form. It's also the embodiment of a quality e.g. the very avatar of kindness. More recently, Avatar has also come to mean a character and/or screen name connected with technology.

For 360 Wisdom purposes, we are going to construct the Avatar in you and to do this takes two stages.

Recall the very first relaxation exercise you completed on page 11.

- CREATE was in your base of your spine.
- FEEL was in your chest.
- THINK was in your head.
- BELIEVE was flowing from your crown throughout your body.

If you were making a character that represented a Creative, what qualities would they have? e.g. imaginative, expressive, witty. (You can look back to some of the qualities in the Healthy Range for CREATE on page 45) to help you identify some.

Now, can you turn this into a character and give him/her an identity or name? e.g. poet, patisserie maker, story-teller, designer.

Do the same for all the other Quarters. Here's an example of what you could end up with.

- CREATE = imaginative, amusing, inventive = The Story-teller.
- FEEL = caring, passionate, generous. = The Romantic.
- THINK = rational, detailed, thoughtful. = The Philosopher.
- BELIEVE = compassionate, other-worldly, idealistic = The Mystic.

Imagine how each of these characters looks, moves and sounds. Picture/feel each one of them in you.

- Base of the spine = The Story-teller.
- Chest = The Romantic.
- Head = The Philosopher.
- Crown through whole body = The Mystic.

Now, feel the characters move inside you until they come together into one form and find a resting place inside you. (You may need to do this several times to get them in the correct place for you and they may end up somewhere you didn't expect!)

Write down here where they reside in you. This is your Avatar. Your Avatar 'locks in' these archetypes. If you can give your Avatar substance through a name, a personality, a form, even better!

My Avatar is ______________________________

As you move forward in life, never forget these 360 Wise characters are locked into you in this place as your Avatar. Feel their combined power. Use them to guide you and act as the source of your wisdom, comfort and inspiration and rationale. When you have a decision to make, they will enable you to steer a true course.

4 I Am...

Turn to the Essence Statement you created on page 58 and your True Values on page 61. Look at them carefully with your Avatar's gaze.

Can you see a trail running through your Essence Statement and True Values?

Here are some examples to help you:

Carol's Essence Statement is 'I enjoy making things grow from nothing.' Her True Values are creativity, connectivity, authenticity. When her Avatar came together, she called her 'Power'. Power is located in her hands.

Carol was able to encapsulate all of this into one sentence she uses to keep her centered and on track with her life. It is 'I am a powerful creator.'

Bridget's Essence Statement is 'I am the crop that keeps the hungry nourished' because of her role on the plantation and her desire to leave a legacy to help young people follow in her footsteps. Her True Values are faith, aspiration and integrity.

When her Avatar came together, she called her 'Hope'. Hope is located in her eyes.
Bridget was able to encapsulate all of this into one sentence: 'I am the bountiful provider.'
Name your Avatar and imagine what he/she looks like.

Now, stand and take yourself through the 360 Relaxation exercise (making sure your diving boots are firmly anchored!).

When you feel completely present and relaxed, transfer your image down into the palm of your stronger hand. Imagine you are throwing a javelin in the same hand and release your image with the throw knowing you are sending it far, far into space to the stars.

Your Essence Image is waiting to greet you at your journey's end, shining like a light.

Time on the Crystal

By understanding how you THINK and FEEL, you have reconsidered and reworked your past. You have learned to CREATE and BELIEVE in the future. As a result, time has been fused together and become one through the Crystallisation Process. You are now prepared for the journey across time and space, for your Essence Image awaits you at your destination.

Before you enter the Diamond, you are going to test your ability to travel at this speed so you can manage going beyond known time into *simultaneous* time! This is the speed of light.

Relax and imagine the sun is shining inside your forehead. It is radiating a warm, gentle heat that gradually moves down your body. As it does, you will feel relaxed, safe and loved. The sun moves down your arms and into your chest, calming your beating heart and filling it with warmth; down through your stomach, pelvis, legs, throbbing gently through your feet, ending as two sunbeams in your right and left little toes.

Imagine you are blowing them out of your body with a gentle 'huff' so the beams float like dandelion seeds to the next person who is waiting to relax.

Now, you feel totally at peace with crystal-strong stability.

Imagine you are looking up to see the sun shining above you high in the sky. Don't look directly into it, for it is so bright, it may blind you. What you can see clearly though are the sunbeams shining down from the sun's heart. Choose a sunbeam and step on it. Allow it to lift you and travel upwards along its shaft. As you travel nearer to the sun, you feel its heat, but it's not unbearable. Instead, its warmth is tender and kind. You move closer until you enter the centre of the sun. You pass through it, noticing your physical body and mind is intact, but your emotions are smouldering. Your hate, passion, anger, fear, sadness, jealousy, happiness all erupt into flames, burning up as you pass through the sun. As you bathe in the flames, it is as if all past feelings have been reduced to ashes so you arrive on the other side of the sun cleansed and purified.

The fire has set you free.

The only emotion remaining is love, a love so profound for you and all living things, it is unconditional.

From this moment, you commit to using your whole-being, 360-self for the good of the planet.

Now, look around you. There are no stars or planets. There is no light and darkness. Here, you exist in 'no time' in a place called 'No-space'. It's a physical space which is completely empty and at the same time it is full. This is because it is pregnant with possibility and prospects. Here, you can consider things in total peace and dispassion. Nothing here can harm you. You are totally safe. You are totally aware. You are 360. It's time to make a difference. You are ready to meet your destiny.

You see a diamond shining in the space. Stand on it and let its light shine through you.

Section Eight: DIAMOND

"Invest in the human soul. Who knows, it might be a diamond in the rough."
(Mary McLeod Bethune.)

The strength of the diamond is legendary. It has an almost perfect atomic structure and is the closest thing to a clear physical substance in existence. (If you stood next to a diamond wall, you wouldn't see it.) It is the strongest known material in the universe.

The Diamond sits in the centre of the 360 Wisdom Circle.

The Diamond makes living in human time and all the associated worries about coping, managing, fixing, getting ahead, all fade into insignificance as they are over-shadowed by something of greater meaning and worth.

The Diamond has two main qualities which are described in more detail below:

- It has 'Field Intelligence'. (This refers to a higher consciousness as described by mystics and sages throughout the ages.)
- It works simultaneously in time and dimensions of reality/space.

Field Intelligence

In 1964, Physicist John Bell[28] had an idea known as 'Bell's Theory'. He believed that all objects and events in the universe respond to each others change of state. If a star dies out millions of light years away from the earth, somewhere else in the cosmos, another one is born. This implies that the 'field' knows how to organise matter and intelligence to give it form.

Simultaneous Time and Space

This 'Field' is known in Quantum Physics as the sub-atomic or Quantum world. Beyond the atom and its constituent parts (protons, neutrons, electrons) and the smallest matter identified so far (quarks), is a lot of space. If you crushed all known matter together in the universe, it would compress down to something the size of a very, very heavy squash ball. The rest of the universe is made up of empty space. 99.9999% of an atom consists of nothing!

It's believed that this space I call the 'Field' holds all of reality together. David Bohm[28] took Bell's Theory one stage further by suggesting the 'Field' has a kind of **knowing** what is happening everywhere *at once*. It is as if the 'Field' is nowhere and everywhere instantly. The 'Field' has no concept of the system we have created for measuring intervals in time. There is no measuring here, no past, present or future. Everything operates simultaneously in one, some or all spatial dimensions.

We can communicate with the 'Field' and get a response. But often we don't realise what we're doing and put its effects down to coincidence, luck or chance. Now you know that an intelligence exists, you will also realise that when you communicate with it and things change around you, you will put this down to your ability to create and design just like the 'Field' does because you are in it. All of the work you have done in 360 Wisdom has been to put you in touch with the 'Field'.

Because the 'Field' is all around us (and in us as you will learn in the next paragraph), it's quite difficult to visualise what it *is*. Our senses scream out wanting to experience the thing and that is not possible with today's technology. It is only a matter of time before we are able to measure and experience the ''Field' if science continues apace.

So, for now, imagine the 'Field' is a giant server and each one of us is a PC that can communicate over space and time with it.

You are about to learn how to communicate with it and use the possibilities that come from the 'Field' to realise your potential for the benefit of all living things.

Mind-Body Intelligence

If the 'Field' is out there in space, is it in us? The answer is **YES**. You learned in FEEL that we know there is a biological communicating system as well as the classically known electrical/ nervous system. Neuroscientists have discovered (and still continue to find out more) that the brain has chemical neurotransmitters and they can be found throughout the body. Our 'body-mind' can communicate simultaneously with itself. The neurotransmitters push the thought out and with it goes a chemical that produces a cascade of responses at a cellular level throughout the body's 'inner-space' and the type of receptor on the cell it's intended for will receive it and cause the cell to take a range of actions e.g. growing, changing, dying, to change its function. This has profound implications for wellness and illness in us and has been taken one step further in the new field of epigenetics. Bruce Lipton[29] suggests that genes and DNA do not control our body, but that signals from outside the cell in the form of energetic messages emanating from our positive and negative thoughts do.

It isn't a great step of imagination to see that if what is inside us and outside of us is one and the same, we need a switch we can flick to connect the two. 360 in its entirety can be this switch.

The Key: You, the Observer

So, if our inner-space is identical to the outer space in the 'Field', we have been communicating throughout our body-mind (but maybe more sub-consciously than consciously). If we can consciously know the impact of our thoughts on our body-mind (THINK and FEEL have focused on helping you do this), why not try to use the same processes to communicate with the 'Field'?

The key to all inner and outer-world communication is **YOU**. You are the intelligence and it is the same as the 'Field's' intelligence, just a little smaller!

Note here to not confuse what you know about the material world with the 'Field'. You will not be doing mind over matter in the classical sense (moving objects with thought). Your 'mindful' thoughts will be consciously put from you simultaneously into the 'Field', setting up a series of possibilities and changes that will come back out of the 'Field' into your reality, altering it accordingly. The more you engage with the 'Field', the better your results will become. Practice makes perfect! As Thomas Edison, the Inventor once said "*"I know this world is ruled by infinite intelligence. Everything that surrounds us- everything that exists proves that there are infinite laws behind it. There can be no denying this fact. It is mathematical in its precision"* [30].

To switch yourself on, you need to be 360 and in the *mindful* state. Then, issue a communication to the 'Field' and let it go into it. (We will do this in the 'Opening the Field' section with the WISDOM technique.)

You then need to shift into the *'Observer State'*. This state is similar to mindfulness (see section 'Quieting the Mind' on page 28 and repeat the exercise to reacquaint yourself with the concept of 'Mindfulness'.) The Observer State has no expectations, pre-conditions, premonitions, It just *is*. You are present, awake and mindful and are observing your human self watching, engaging and moving in the world. After you have released your WISDOM into the 'Field', get on with the business of living – but continue to watch out for the subtle signs, messages and 'coincidences' that manifest around you. Then you take action.

"You observe and observe and let this experience well up into something appropriate. In a sense, there's no decision-making. What you do just becomes obvious. You can't rush it. Much of it depends on where you're coming from and who you are as a person. All you can do is position yourself according to your unfolding vision of what is coming. A totally different set of rules applies. You need to 'feel out' what to do." Peter Senge[31].

Use your peripheral vision, your 360 Wisdom to notice and understand the messages and material things that occur as you change your reality and reality around you. Energy, ideas, possibilities and inspiration to do extraordinary things will come as you access energy, making something new from it, a true alchemist.

You will soon see a clear pathway. Follow it. The messages, information, 'co-incidences' and opportunities will only get stronger! The diagram below shows you the Field Communication Process. The 360 Wisdom Guide enables you to become balanced and centered in the Temporal World i.e. the material world we live in today. Once you are 360, you can apply the WISDOM technique and all you have learned to open the 'Field' inside and outside of you i.e. to communicate with the 'Field' (in the diagram below, this is the second circle called the Quantum Field). Once you begin to understand the language of the 'Field' and can create within it, you move into the third circle, called the 'Unified Field'. This is a completely different landscape and *modus operandi*. The 'Unified Field' will be the subject of a future 360 Wisdom publication.

Opening the Field

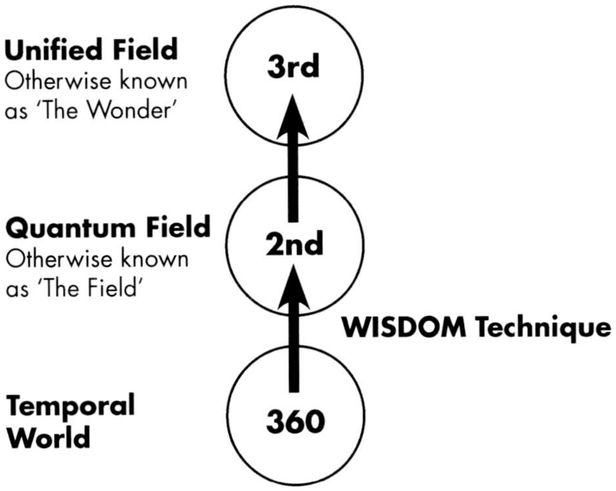

You can open the 'Field' using the WISDOM technique to move from the temporal world into the 'Field.'

There are three preparatory actions before you use WISDOM.

The First Action
Get into the 360 perspective and stand on the Diamond. (If you can visualise yourself doing this, even better.)

The Second Action
Be focused on your essence and what you want to achieve for the world and its greater good. Stay detached from the action as the Observer.

The Third Action
Complete WISDOM and then go with what comes out of the 'Field'. (For this exercise you can use the WISDOM sheets on page 82.)

W **WISH**

Work out what you want to realise in the future. (As a starting point, use some of the actions you put on your postcards). Take your time to compose this carefully so that you create positive imprints. Write what you want in a short paragraph on the WISDOM sheet. Keep asking yourself: "Is there another way? Have I got this right?"

I **IMAGINE**

Holding the WISDOM sheet in your hands, imagine what the final outcome will look like/ feel like/sound like. How will it benefit others, who will be helped and what difference will it make in yours and their lives.

S **SENSE**

Use all your senses to understand the feelings people have. What are the smells, sights, touch, tastes of the experience you have created?

D **DECIDE**

A final check to make sure all is done from 360 Wisdom. Make sure you have considered your THINK and FEEL patterns and your creation fits with your CREATE, your values and BELIEVE. Check it is in the Healthy Range.

O **OBJECTIFY**

As you did with your Essence Statement, 'throw' your WISDOM into the 'Field' true and straight like a javelin.

Now, imagine you are standing in the place far away in space where you sent your Essence Statement. Look back from here and watch the javelin speeding towards you. It lands at your feet. Look back at its trajectory and note all the things that have happened, (you may sense these in clear pictures, impressions, sounds, feelings) and note them. They are your stepping stones across the 'Field'.

M **MAKE (HAPPEN)**

You may be able to action a lot of the stepping stones yourself. Some will resolve themselves and/or other people will help you. Write down any impressions you have and turn them into an action plan with the headings, *by when/date, resources needed* and *measures of success*. Return to your action plan to refine it and add/remove actions as required.

The more you practice the WISDOM technique, the stronger the links between your inner intelligence and the 'Field' intelligence will become. (Imagine a drop of water becoming a stream then a flow, then a river and then a sea.) The more you practice 360 WISDOM, the stronger the links become.

"Your beliefs become your thoughts. Your thoughts become your words. Your words become your actions. Your actions become your habits. Your habits become your values. Your values become your destiny." [32]

Closing the Field

Field communication is a great power to possess. The final thing to do is to close your link to the 'Field' when you are not consciously using it. The unconscious mind is very powerful and works in a really simplistic way. (For example, it takes in messages quite literally and focuses on key words. So if you say to yourself 'I don't want to be ill', your subconscious is likely to hear 'want to be ill.') There are ways you can re-pattern your use of language to correct much of this e.g. Neuro-linguistic programming[33] If you don't close down your link to the 'Field', what comes out of the 'Field' might not be understood, predicted or planned for.

Please Close the Field With This Visualisation

You are standing in front of a stone temple.

The 360 Wisdom Circle turns in the entrance, spinning faster and faster until its colours turn white. A diamond light flows from the circle creating steps, each one the colour of the rainbow.

Let us climb those steps together.

RED	I am happy with myself and put myself into others perspectives.
ORANGE	I create ideas, I imagine, I dream of better things.
YELLOW	I use my power for the good of the planet and its living beings.
GREEN	I work from my heart. I care deeply about others.
BLUE	I speak truth and say what I mean, mean what I say, do what I say.
INDIGO	I work from my intuition and higher-self.
VIOLET	I am a part and at one in 'the Field'. I know how to create and direct energy from myself for the good of all.
	I am crystal clear.

We enter a large room with a vaulted ceiling. In the centre, is a statue of a woman. Sitting in her lap is a large diamond.

The colours of the rainbow shine from it too. You touch the diamond and make a wish. Wait. It will come to you. Use it wisely.

As you practice 360 Wisdom, communication with the 'Field' becomes easier. You will see changes in your life and your relationships with yourself and others. Life will become richer and enriched. You will understand the unity and connection with all living things. You will feel unbridled joy and unconditional love.

As you move into the 'Unified Field' 360 Wisdom: The Wonder World awaits!

References

(1)	John M Richardson Jnr.	www.thinkexist.com
(2)	Anthony De Mello SJ	*Awareness*. Page 5. Fount Paperbacks.
(3)	William Shakespeare	*Hamlet*. Act IIIi The Arden Shakespeare, Methuen.
(4)	Debbie Ford	*The Shadow Effect*. DVD. Hay House.
(5)	Dr. Morris Massey	www.changingminds.org
(6)	Alfred Korzybski	www.gestalt.org/alfred.htm
(7)	Ronnie Lessem	*Developing in Phases*. Ch19. *Creative Management*. (Ed. Jane Henry), Open University/Sage Publications.
(8)	Candace B. Pert PHD	*Molecules of Emotion*. Pages 136-7 Simon & Schuster UK Ltd.
(9)	Geshe Michael Roach	*The Diamond Cutter*. Pages 68 & 80. Doubleday.
(10)	Alexandra Massey	www.alexandramassey.co.uk
(11)	Thich Nhat Hanh	*Anger: Buddhist Wisdom for Cooling the Flames*. Rider Books
(12)	Daniel Goleman	*Emotional Intelligence & Working with Emotional Intelligence* (Omnibus) Bloomsbury.
(13)	Tony Buzan	*The Power of Creative Intelligence* page 13. Thorsons.
(14)	Creative process	Jane Henry. *Making Sense of Creativity* Ch1 page 7 *Creative Management* (Ed. Jane Henry), Open University/Sage Publications.
(15)	James Dyson	*Against the Odds*, Orion Business Publishing.
(16)	Charles Handy	*The Age of Unreason* Ch20. *Creative Management* (Ed. Jane Henry), Open University/Sage Publications.
(17)	Engines of our Ingenuity	www.uh.edu/engines/epi265.htm
(18)	American Museum of Natural History	www.amnh.org/exhibitions/einstein/light/index.php
(19)	Tony Buzan	*The Power of Creative Intelligence* page 13. Thorsons.
(20)	Betty Edwards	www.drawright.com/
(21)	Edward De Bono	www.edwdebono.com/
(22)	Oprah Winfrey	www.oprah.com/spirit/Oprahs-Private-Journals-Diary-Excerpts
(23)	Richard Branson	www.centreforthemind.com/images/BransonTranscript%20.pdf
(24)	Jane Henry	*Making Sense of Creativity* Ch1. *Creative Management* (Ed. Jane Henry), Open University/Sage Publications.
(25)	Danah Zohar & Ian Marshall	*Spiritual Capital: Wealth We Can Live By*. Pages 96-7. Bloomsbury.
(26)	Michel de Montaigne	*Essays*, 1580. www.quotegarden.com/dreams.html
(27)	Erkhart Tolle.	*The Power of Now*. Page 14 Hodder & Stoughton.
(28)	Depak Chopra	*Quantum Healing* pages 104-5. Bantam Books.
(29)	Bruce H. Lipton PHD.	*The Biology of Belief*. Hay House.
(30)	Thomas Edison	www.brainyquote.com/quotes/authors/t/thomas_a_edison.html
(31)	Peter Senge & C. Otto Scharmer & Joseph Jaworsky & Betty Sue Flowers	*Presence*. Nicholas Brealey.
(32)	Mahatma Gandhi	www.quotationspage.com/quote/36464.html
(33)	NLP	en.wikipedia.org/wiki/Neurolinguistic_programming

Blank Pages for Readers to use

Aha Moments

Actions of Kindness

Things to Create

WISDOM Sheets

Record of Success

People and Books That Have Inspired Me

The Way of the Wizard	Deepak Chopra Rider
Against the Odds	James Dyson Orion
Awareness	Anthony De Mello Fount
One From Many	Dee Hock Berrett-Koehler
In Search of the Miraculous	PD Ouspensky Routledge & Keegan Paul
Presence	Peter Senge & C. Otto Scharmer & Joseph Jaworsky & Betty Sue Flowers Nicholas Brealey
The Diamond Cutter	Geshe Michael Roche Doubleday
Banker to the Poor	Muhammad Yunus Aurium
The Art of Possibility	Rosamund Stone Zander & Ben Zander Penguin
Spiritual Intelligence *The Ultimate Intelligence*	Danah Zohar & Ian Marshall Bloomsbury